Temitope (Tope) has been forged by the storms and trials of life for this: to bless others with what she, herself, received. To pass on the encouragement and hope she found in those dark times to others. When life gets hard, God is there. His love is there. His comfort is there. His support is there. And sometimes it takes an experienced guide to help us find that love, comfort, and support again. Tope is that guide. She has weathered the storms and endured the trials to help us with ours. Thank you, Tope, for taking the time to encourage us with the care you have received from Him.

~Pastor Mike Green
LifeSpring Church, Durham, North Carolina

Every person who breathes will walk through storms that seem like they will never end. Tope's book not only brings hope that the sun will shine again, it shows us how to find God's blessings in the midst of the storm. She has personally survived terrible storms in life, but she has thrived and has chosen to share her experience and wisdom with us.

~Ken Davis
Author, speaker, communications trainer

Dr. Temitope Keku's experience and wisdom is like the calm in the storm for her readers. In the midst of life disturbances, her devotional is a safe place to breathe, focus, and discover the riches of God's promises. I'll recommend *Weathering Storms: Finding Treasures in the Ruins* to my coaching clients as a resource for encouragement and hope.

~Lori Boruff
Life coach, speaker, Christian Communicators co-director
Author of *Hope in the Ruins: A Rescue and Recovery Plan for Hearts in Crisis*

Temitope is a master storyteller. Our generation needs elders who help us to see ourselves and gain insights through the art of storytelling. Temitope wants us to understand that life is a series of unfolding events that reveal gems to lighten our hearts and brighten our way. When you read this book, you find yourself in the stories, and you catch a glimpse of how God shows up for and with you!

~Sackeena Gordon-Jones, PhD, MCC
Chief coaching officer of Transformation Edge Coaching & Consulting
Coach training and coaching services for leaders and organizations

WEATHERING Storms

To Ms. Bea,

I have come that they
may have life and have it
more abundantly. John 10:10

May you experience God's
abundance in every situation.

Blessings,

Tope

WEATHERING Storms

Finding Treasures in the Ruins

Dr. Temitope Keku

ROMANS 8:28
BOOKS

Weathering Storms: Finding Treasures in the Ruins

Published by Redemption Press, PO Box 427, Enumclaw, WA 98022.

Toll-Free (844) 2REDEEM (273-3336)

Redemption Press is honored to present this title in partnership with the author. The views expressed or implied in this work are those of the author. Redemption Press provides our imprint seal representing design excellence, creative content, and high -quality production.

For more information on this book and the author, visit: www.hiddentreasuresandriches.com.

Library of Congress Cataloging-in-Publication Data
Keku, Dr. Temitope
Weathering Storms: Finding Treasures in the Ruins / Dr. Temitope Keku 1st ed.

ISBN: 978-1-68314-888-3
Hard: 978-1-68314-891-3
Epub: 978-1-68314-889-0
Mobi: 978-1-68314-890-6

LCCN: 2019910595

Table of Contents

Identity

Forgiveness

Intimacy with God

Hope in the Storm

Gratitude

Dedication

To my parents,

Samuel and Janet Akinyele

Thank you for shining your light
and igniting my faith.
The practical lessons you taught me
and my siblings about God
live on after you.

Acknowledgments

I am eternally indebted to the many people who made this book possible. My heartfelt gratitude to Lori Boruff for inspiring me to stay the course. She coached me through difficult challenges when I was stuck and helped me envision the finished devotional and the opportunity it would provide to inspire others to embrace hope.

I also acknowledge the support of Michelle Viscuse, my writing buddy, for her valuable feedback and accountability. I am indebted to Andrea Merrell for giving care and thought to every word, paragraph, and page to make the manuscript better. To Athena Dean Holtz, Hanna McKenzie, Dori Harrell, Maryna Zhukova, Judy Hagey, and the Redemption Press staff—thank you for making it possible to share my message. God bless you.

A shout-out to all my friends, especially Carol Schellenberg and the ladies in my small group who cheered me on through their prayers.

A special thank-you to my husband and children for their unconditional love and encouragement. You are my special treasures. Without you and the experiences we share, I could not have written this devotional.

Finally, I am grateful to the almighty God, who loves me more than I can ever imagine. When troubles and challenges overwhelmed me, your constant presence was a source of strength. You showed me how to stand, trust, and mine for hidden treasures in the storms. Thank you, Papa. You are my greatest treasure and the reason for my hope.

It is in the **quiet crucible**

of your personal, private sufferings

that your **noblest dreams** are born

and God's **greatest gifts** are given.

WINTLEY PHIPPS

Preface

The storms of life often throw us for a loop and can leave us feeling deflated, stuck, and without options. These storms come in a myriad of forms, such as relationship failures, family dysfunction, financial problems, job loss, or health issues.

If we try to weather our storm alone, we will end up frustrated. When we are going through tough times, we need hope. We need an anchor to pull us through the raging storms. What is often missing is how to translate our knowledge of God and apply it to our storms, which often appear larger than life.

I have been through many storms, and sometimes the storms seemed stronger than my faith. But when I allowed Jesus into my storms, my fears took a backseat. God's faithfulness during my trials has sustained me and shaped my outlook.

Weathering Storms: Finding Treasures in the Ruins will help you gain godly insights in your situations and give you hope. Life's storms usually contain hidden treasures, and this devotional will inspire you to discover the hidden treasures of intimacy with God: identity, patience, peace, forgiveness, gratitude, and hope in your adversity.

As you seek God's perspective, you will gain clarity, hope, and peace. The real-life stories and examples of men and women in the Bible will encourage you to stand strong, trust God, and not be overwhelmed by your circumstances. You will discover that knowing your identity in Christ and God's love for you are important elements to overcoming adversity.

It is my prayer that no matter what your storm is about, this book will provide hope and practical guidance for weathering your storm well.

Identity

God Loves You Personally and Passionately

For we are God's masterpiece.
He has created us anew in Christ Jesus,
so we can do the good things
he planned for us long ago
EPHESIANS 2:10 NLT

During a mission trip to Ethiopia, I planned to talk to the women on their identity in Christ, but I was unsure how to illustrate it in a culturally relevant way. During one service, a woman gave me a milk jug made from a gourd and beautifully decorated with colored beads. When I saw the milk jug, I knew it would be an excellent illustration for my message.

I shared with the women that just as the artist who made the beautiful milk jug took great care, God took great care to create each of us and considers us his masterpieces. He created and designed us to do good works, which he planned long ago and equipped us with purpose, unique gifts, and talents.

I then asked each woman to repeat after me: "God loves (insert your name)." It moved many of the women to tears, but they were tears of joy. Afterward, I found out they had never considered that God knew them personally and loved them passionately. I reminded them, no matter the challenges we face, nothing can separate us from God's love.

Like my friends in Ethiopia, Jesus loves you unconditionally. His thoughts toward you are precious and are not dependent on your life's circumstances. When God thinks of you, he sees you as precious in many ways. He fully knows you, just as he knows each star by name. "How precious to me are your thoughts, O God! How vast is the sum of them! If I would count them, they are more than the sand. I awake, and I am still with you" (Psalm 139:7–8 ESV).

What keeps us from embracing God's love? Jesus paid the price on the cross so that all who come to him receive forgiveness, love, and assurance of eternal life. Imagine what your life could be like if you invite him in and accept his unconditional love. You are beautifully and wonderfully made—a masterpiece. He loves you.

Prayer

Thank you, Lord,
for taking great care to create me
and for the assurance of your love.
Amen.

Remember Who You Are

*God made him who had no sin
to be sin for us, so that in him
we might become the righteousness of God.*
2 CORINTHIANS 5:21

I had an assignment I kept putting off. Every time I thought about it, I felt a sense of dread. I could not understand why I was feeling so much resistance toward completing this assignment. I had done similar work before and did fine.

Somehow, I bought in to the Enemy's lies and let him convince me I could not complete this assignment. The deadline was near, and I was at my wits' end. Finally, I went to the Lord in prayer. As I sat there contemplating the work, the Lord whispered to my heart, *You are the righteousness of God in Christ.*

Those words put a fire in my belly. Suddenly, I had clarity on how to proceed with the assignment, and I completed it by the deadline.

That day, 2 Corinthians 5:21 took on a completely new meaning. The Enemy is crafty, and his goal is to put obstacles in our way. To push through the resistance requires us to remember who we are in Christ. The Enemy is determined to sabotage us, but we don't have to fall for his tactics.

When we remember who we are in Christ and confront the Enemy with God's truth, his tactics lose their grip. When Jesus was in the wilderness, fasting for forty days and forty nights, Satan knew he was hungry, so he asked Jesus to command the stones to turn into bread. Jesus confronted him with God's truth: "It is written, man shall not live by bread alone but on every word that comes from the mouth of God" (Matthew 4:4).

Memorizing and meditating on Scripture is a useful tool that has helped me in several sticky situations. When we face temptation or feel overwhelmed, we need not fear, because God is with us. He will bring those Scriptures we have hidden in our heart to mind so we can confront the Enemy with truth. Most importantly, God can use the Scripture to remind us of who we are.

Remember who you are: a child of God and the righteousness of God in Christ. Press through the resistance, persevere, and trust the Lord to help you.

Prayer

Lord, help me meditate on your truth
so that when I face opposition,
I can stand strong and remember
who I am in you.
Amen.

Secure in God's Strength

She is clothed with strength and dignity,
and she laughs without fear of the future.
PROVERBS 31:25 NLT

It was a busy Saturday. Our plans for the day included taking kids to soccer practice, piano lessons, and a birthday party. My daughter's friend Lauren invited her to a birthday party. Because my son also had a friend named Lauren, I misunderstood who was invited to the party.

I rushed home to drop off one kid and picked up my son to go to the birthday party. To my horror, only girls were at the party. I took the wrong kid to the party, and I was embarrassed.

Working full time, being a mom, and maintaining a household is challenging. Regardless, I apologized to Lauren's mom and my children. I felt bad about the incident.

For years, I have admired the woman described in Proverbs 31. I wondered how she could be efficient, organized, and accomplish so much. She was intentional, hardworking, managed her home and resources wisely, and was kind and respected. As I studied her life, I understood why she could laugh at the future. The Proverbs 31 woman did not have time to fret over her inadequacies. She recognized God as the source of her strength and dignity. She clothed herself daily in his righteousness and did not fear or worry about the future. I believe knowing God as her security was the source of her confidence.

When we make mistakes, we can become vulnerable to Satan's

accusations and condemnation. The Bible calls him a thief and a liar whose main goal is to steal, kill, and destroy. He goes after our joy, dignity, and strength.

How do we deter him? The life of the Proverbs 31 woman provides valuable insights. Embracing our identity in Christ is key to walking in authority and confidence. An approach that helps me clothe myself in God's strength and dignity is to meditate on Scriptures about my identity every morning. I write these Scriptures on notecards and place them on the mirror in my bathroom. I dress up in them while getting ready for the day.

You, too, can know Jesus as the source of your strength, dignity, and confidence.

Prayer

Lord, life can be challenging at times.
Thank you for clothing me
with strength and dignity in Jesus.
Amen.

Holy and Blameless without Condemnation

He has brought you into his own presence,
and you are holy and blameless
as you stand before him without a single fault.
But you must continue to believe this truth
and stand firmly in it.

COLOSSIANS 1:22–23 NLT

When I went through a crisis in my marriage, one area the Enemy attacked relentlessly was my identity. I felt shame, fear, and condemnation, yet I couldn't understand why I felt this way. I blamed myself for the situation in my marriage.

Do you ever struggle with these issues?

The Enemy is the father of lies. His tactics cause us to fear and doubt, make us feel unsettled, and move us away from the hope of Jesus. He wants to make us unsteady and distracted by his lies. He causes us to question our worth.

If you find yourself fearful and questioning your identity, Colossians 1:22–23 is a lifeline straight from the Father to you and me. Pause and reflect on these truths and let them sink into your soul.

God makes it clear in these verses that we have nothing to be ashamed of because Jesus gave himself on the cross for our sins and shortcomings. By his death, he removed our fears, shame, and condemnation. He declared us blameless and without condemnation.

The best part of this truth is that we don't earn it or deserve it. Neither is it defined by our circumstances or the size of the storm we are facing. Christ gave himself up for us to present us without stain or wrinkle or any other blemish, holy and blameless (Ephesians 5:27). Our identity is a gift we receive from the Father when we declare our faith in Jesus.

Prayer

Father, thank you for reminding me
that my identity is deeply rooted
in the finished work of Jesus Christ.
Help me stay grounded
in the truth of your Word
that I am holy and blameless in your sight.
Amen.

He Knows My Name

Look up into the heavens.
Who created all the stars?
He brings them out like an army,
one after another, calling each by its name.
Because of his great power and incomparable strength,
not a single one is missing.

ISAIAH 40:26 NLT

It was pitch dark as we sat under the open skies in rural Ethiopia. The beautiful night sky twinkled with hundreds of stars. As people arrived, they sat on the ground in circles, waiting to watch the *Jesus* movie. While the movie was playing, I could not help but focus on the stars and the majesty of the Creator.

As I looked at the crescent-shaped moon and the stars, I was humbled to know that God, the Creator of the universe, knows my name. He also knows the name of each person who was watching the movie, just like he knows each star by name. Quietly I marveled at the Lord's majesty and praised his greatness. My heart was encouraged because he knows my name and he sees me.

I am known.

Sitting in this crowd, I felt like I was alone with God. I experienced a warm glow over my heart as I lifted my eyes and offered prayers of praise and adoration to the One who knows about my trials. I thanked him for his goodness and for his wonderful creation: the stars, the moon, sea creatures, birds, and all animals.

In that moment, all I could think of was his love and his presence all around me. My heart was full as I joined the stars to praise him. That night I recognized that the size of my storm does not have to overwhelm me if I am willing to shift my gaze.

Friend, God knows your name. You can rest assured that He cares about you and your situation. He doesn't get tired or grow weary. In his presence, our challenges fade as we trust him to hold our hands. Because of God's great love and power, we don't have to allow our trials to overwhelm us. We can trust him because he knows everything about us (Psalm 139:1–2).

Prayer

Lord, when I consider your majesty and power,
I stand in awe
Thank you for the stars and your beautiful creation.
Thank you for creating me in your own image.
I rest secure in your love.
The assurance that you know my name
gives me comfort and hope.
Amen.

Remember Your True Identity

See what great love the Father has lavished on us,
that we should be called the children of God!
And that is what we are!

1 JOHN 3:1

A friend and I met for lunch some time ago. During our conversation, she shared how she struggled with approval and acceptance from others. As she shared some painful experiences, I could relate to her. I remembered times when I experienced rejection from loved ones and others close to me.

We all have a need for acceptance, belonging, and love. Rejection hurts deeply and can feel like a blow to our identity. The emotional pain from rejection, especially from loved ones, can leave us with self-doubt, low self-esteem, and depression. It affects our thinking, behavior, and emotions.

Most times, when people reject us, we take their rejection personally. But in reality, their disapproval is usually a reflection of their own brokenness and hurts. So rather than question our identity, let's embrace who we are in Christ. You and I are beloved children of God, blessed and highly favored, chosen, lavishly loved, accepted, significant, and secure (Ephesians 1:3–14).

Our identity and security are in God's unchanging love for us. It does not depend on our performance or other people's approval. Jesus endured rejection and shame on the cross so you and I can be free to experience his love and acceptance.

Friend, because of Jesus, you need not struggle with your identity. The Father loves you so much that he went to great lengths to lavish you with his extravagant love. God loves you powerfully and passionately. Remember your true identity!

Imagine God lavishing you with his love as you memorize 1 John 3:1. Recall this verse whenever you are tempted to question your identity.

Prayer

Father, thank you for your extravagant love.
Forgive me for allowing other people's rejection
to cause me to doubt my identity.
Help me remember that
my identity is secure in you.
Amen.

Forgiveness

Ridiculous Mercy

*He has removed our sins as far from us
as the east is from the west.*

PSALM 103:12 NLT

While driving home late one night from visiting a friend, I came across a deer on the road. I slowed down, hoping the deer would move on, but it stood there as if stuck in a daze. I did not want to hit it, so I waited until it was safe to go around it on the other lane.

Have you ever felt like that deer, stuck in a daze and unable to move? *Why did I experience a heap of condemnation when I failed again to meet the deadline? What is wrong with me? Why couldn't I do this simple thing?* Condemnation is one of Satan's tools to keep us paralyzed, guilty, and unproductive.

Relief filled me when I read God's view of our shortcomings and failures in Psalm 103:8–12. God is compassionate, overflowing with mercy, grace, and rich love. He does not nag us continuously or hold a grudge against us. Better yet, he does not even treat us as our sins deserve or pay us back in full for our wrongs. He separates us from our sins as far as the east is from the west. Friend, this is the definition of ridiculous mercy.

Perhaps you struggle when you do not meet a deadline, pay a debt, love others, or honor your spouse. The good news is that God will never condemn or shame us for our failures. When we turn to him and ask for forgiveness, he is faithful to forgive us, and it does not depend on our performance. God has a broad view of our failures, because he doesn't see us as we are. He sees what we can

become. God's mercy toward you and me is ridiculous.
How have you experienced God's ridiculous mercy?

Prayer

Lord, your love doesn't depend
on my performance.
Thank you for forgiving my shortcomings
and for your overflowing mercy.
Thank you that I am eternally redeemed
and completely forgiven.
Amen.

Dealing with Negative Emotions

But she said to her,
"Wasn't it enough that you took away my husband?
Will you take my son's mandrakes too?"
GENESIS 30:15

Anger is a common emotion we all experience during times of trials. We can feel justified by our anger because others wrong us. Anger handled improperly can lead to negative emotions such as discouragement, hatred, and depression. It causes friction and disunity in families.

Leah weathered the storm of rejection and hostility from her dad, sister, and husband. Nobody noticed her fine qualities or inner beauty. All they saw was her weak eye. She had every reason to be angry. Living with constant tension and strife was a norm.

How did Leah handle her anger and painful emotions? She didn't wish them away or pretend she wasn't hurt. Though it took a while, she turned to God with her pain. In time, God blessed her with children. The names of her children reflect her progressive understanding of God's love for her.

"Leah became pregnant and gave birth to a son. She named him Reuben, for she said, 'It is because the Lord has seen my misery'" (Genesis 29:32). She thought the birth of her son would make her husband love her. Then she gave birth to another son and named him Simeon, which means, "one who hears." Her third son she named Levi. When her fourth son was born, she named him Judah, which means "praise" (Genesis 29:32–35).

How do you handle negative emotions?

If we are not careful, the devil can use anger to quench our spirit and drive a wedge between us and the Holy Spirit. We can be angry but not sin. "Do not let the sun go down while you are still angry, and do not give the devil a foothold" (Ephesians 4:26–27).

When I feel angry, I tell God about it. Honest expression of my feelings and emotions is important to my well-being and spiritual health. Sometimes I ask a trustworthy mentor or friend to pray with me. Other times I seek the help of professional counselors to help me process my emotions.

Our emotions don't have to control us if we will acknowledge them and bring them under the Holy Spirit's control. Like Leah, as I work through my emotions, I shift my focus to God's acceptance of me.

Prayer

My emotions can feel overwhelming
and make me want to lash out at others.
Lord, help me yield my emotions to your control
as you work to produce
the character of Jesus in me.
Amen.

Giving Grace

Lord, how many times shall I forgive
my brother or sister who sins against me?
Up to seven times?
MATTHEW 18:21

Life is messy. What do you do when people offend you? Do you hold a grudge? Retaliate? People will offend you, and you will offend others. We may feel justified to hold a grudge, but Jesus reminds us there is power and freedom in forgiveness.

In Matthew 18:21–22, Peter asked Jesus, "Lord, how many times shall I forgive my brother or sister who sins against me? Up to seven times?' Jesus answered, 'I tell you, not seven times, but seventy-seven times.'"

During a difficult season in my marriage, I struggled with forgiving my spouse. I was resentful, and I allowed negative emotions to affect my attitude and rob me of joy for a long time. Through much prayer, I surrendered to God as I remembered how much he has forgiven me and still forgives me daily. With God's help, I could forgive.

Nelson Mandela was a political activist in South Africa. He was wrongfully imprisoned for twenty-seven years for protesting segregation. Nelson Mandela could have been bitter and angry. Instead, he came out of prison feeling grateful and empowered. He didn't allow bitterness to hold him hostage as he forgave his adversaries. After his release from prison, he was elected president of South Africa. He facilitated the reconciliation process to help his country heal from the painful effects of segregation. Later, he won the Nobel Prize for peace.

Who do you need to forgive today?

With God's help, you can forgive yourself and others. Unforgiveness is a stronghold that will hold you back from fulfilling your purpose. It is like drinking poison and wishing your enemy would die. Ask God to help you forgive. You may also consider counseling to help you process hard issues. Let go of bitterness and embrace God's freedom!

Prayer

Lord, you command us to forgive.
I confess my struggle
with forgiving myself and others.
I need your help to let go of resentment
and bitterness and embrace your freedom.
Thank you for your grace and mercy
as you forgive me of my sins and shortcomings daily.
Help me to extend grace to others.
Amen.

Unexpected Pardon

He gives justice to the oppressed and food to the hungry.
The Lord frees the prisoners.
PSALM 146:7 NLT

It was an ordinary day on May 13, 1981. Pope John Paul II crossed St. Peter's square as he had done so many times. Suddenly, there was a loud noise that sounded like gunshots. The pope was shot multiple times and sustained life-threatening injuries. The gunman, Mehmet Ali Ağca, an escapee from a Turkish prison, was later apprehended.

Despite his serious injuries, the pope asked all Catholics to pray for the gunman. Ağca was sentenced to life imprisonment by an Italian court for attempted murder. The pope visited his would-be assassin in prison and forgave him.[1]

Stephen was a man of faith who performed great signs and wonders. Some of the Jews and Jewish leaders opposed him and wrongly accused him of blasphemy against Moses and God. They produced false witnesses to testify against Stephen for proclaiming his faith in Jesus. As he walked them through God's plan of salvation, beginning with Abraham all the way to Jesus, the Jewish elders became furious, dragged him to the street, and stoned him (Acts 6:8–7:58).

Stephen responded like Pope John Paul II by offering forgiveness to his accusers. As he was dying, Stephen cried out, "Lord, do not hold this sin against them" (Acts 7:60). In 2000, the Pope requested Ağca's pardon. He was released and sent back to Turkey. While serving his previous sentence in Turkey, Ağca became a Christian and was finally set free from prison in 2010.

The pope and Stephen did not allow bitterness and resentment to hold them hostage. They released the offenses and willingly offered unexpected pardon to those who'd wronged them. The pope's forgiveness changed Ağca's life forever. You and I receive forgiveness and unmerited mercy from the Lord daily. He calls us to extend the same mercy to others. When we forgive others, we set them free to experience God's peace and freedom.

How will you respond to those who hurt or offend you? Imagine forgiving that person. In your journal, write what that would look like.

Prayer

When we know and embrace your truth,
we are set free.
Help me be free from the bondage of unforgiveness.
Help me extend your grace to others
as you forgive me of my trespasses.
Amen.

Quiet Desperation

It was not an enemy insulting me.
I could stand that.
It was not someone who hated me.
I could hide from him.
But it is you, a person like me,
my companion and good friend.

PSALM 55:12–13 NCV

Bob and Audrey had it all—a fruitful ministry, a thriving marriage, and a beautiful family. Both were busy with their jobs in ministry and never thought it could happen to them, until adultery snuck in like a thief in the night and shook their marriage to the core. To make matters worse, the adultery resulted in the birth of a child, a constant reminder of this one act of indiscretion.[2]

Forgiveness does not come naturally to any of us. Of all the bad things that can happen, betrayal by a loved one can be the most devastating. If you find yourself in a similar situation, it is understandable to see your spouse as an enemy. Both Bob and Audrey struggled with feeling unlovable toward each other. Audrey felt horrible after she confessed to the affair.

The prophet Hosea also had a messy marriage (Hosea 1–3). His relationship with his wife, Gomer, was extremely challenging. Several times, Gomer went after other men and even bore children by them. Her betrayal and selfishness caused her husband deep pain and anguish (Hosea 2). But she was oblivious to his pain. She enjoyed her irresponsible behavior so much that she wound up in bondage. Hosea had to buy her back. Can you imagine that?

Though Hosea was in a difficult marriage, he loved Gomer through her selfishness, unfaithfulness, and irresponsible behavior (Hosea 3:1–3). The relationship between Hosea and Gomer is a metaphor for our relationship with God. Our waywardness, rebellion, and indiscretions make us enemies of God, but he loves us through it all.

It takes time to process the emotional pain and physical minefields from adultery. Bob forgave his wife and accepted the child. They worked through the process with prayer, community support, and counseling. God restored their marriage. They now share their testimony and give hope to others experiencing infidelity.

If you are dealing with infidelity in your marriage, I understand how difficult it is to forgive an unfaithful spouse. Betrayal inflicts deep emotional pain, anger, confusion, and grief, which can feel like a heavy load. But these emotions need to be addressed in order to have physical and emotional healing. Besides prayer, seek help and support from trusted counselors. This process will take time, but forgiveness is central to healing and restoration.

Are you dealing with the storm of betrayal? How will you ask God to help you through your season of quiet desperation? Trust God with your pain. He specializes in restoring broken ruins.

Prayer

Lord, it is difficult to forgive betrayal
from a close companion.
My heart feels overwhelmed,
and I need your presence, grace, and love
as I process this storm.
Heal my broken heart and help me forgive.
In Jesus's name.
Amen.

Journey to Forgiveness and Freedom

Make allowance for each other's faults,
and forgive anyone who offends you.
Remember, the Lord forgave you,
so you must forgive others.
COLOSSIANS 3:13 NLT

Immaculée Ilibagiza was a young twenty-four-year-old Tutsi college student when war broke out in her home country of Rwanda. Her family was brutally murdered during the Rwandan genocide. She survived because a pastor from the Hutu tribe hid her and seven other women in a tiny bathroom and blocked the door with a wardrobe.

Immaculée felt much bitterness and hatred toward the Hutu men who were killing her tribe. Every time the killers came to the pastor's house, she was torn between her faith in God and her hatred for the killers. She found it difficult to pray.

Then one day, she prayed and asked God to open her heart.

Please open my heart, Lord, and show me how to forgive. I am not strong enough to squash my hatred—they have wronged me so much.... My hatred is so heavy that it could crush me. Touch my heart, Lord, and show me how to forgive.

In that confined bathroom, she repeated this prayer day and night for weeks. One evening, she heard screaming followed by the cry of an infant in the distance. She thought the Hutu men must have killed the baby's mother. Again, hatred and anger welled up in her heart. *How could I forgive people who would do such a thing to an infant?*

Then she heard in her spirit, *You are all my children . . . and the baby is with me now.* After this incident, Immaculée's perspective about the killers changed. She realized that they were God's children who committed barbaric acts but were deserving of love and forgiveness. They were blind men who did not understand that in hurting others they were also hurting themselves.

Immaculée knew she could not ask God to love her if she was unwilling to love the men who hurt her. She asked God to help her forgive. She prayed that God would forgive the killers and lead them to repent.

As her anger drained, she opened her heart, and God touched her with His infinite love. That night for the first time, she slept well. In hiding, Immaculée began the journey to discover deeper faith in God, along with forgiveness and freedom.[3]

In Mark 11:25, the Lord commands us to forgive anyone who offends us so he may forgive our trespasses. Are there people who have deeply hurt you that you find impossible to forgive? How might your inability to forgive affect your prayers?

Prayer

Lord, I lift up those who have treated me unjustly.
Forgive them.
Touch them with your divine love
and help them repent.
Help me not to repay evil for evil
but be an instrument of reconciliation.
Amen.

God's Love Is Deeper Still

*But I tell you, love your enemies
and pray for those who persecute you.*
MATTHEW 5:44

Corrie ten Boom was born in Haarlem, Netherlands. During World War II, Corrie's family helped to save the lives of many Jews. She and her sister, Betsie, were sent to the concentration camp in Ravensbruck, Germany, where they faced untold hardships. Corrie describes her experiences about life in the concentration camp in her book *The Hiding Place*. Corrie's sister died in the camp, but Corrie was miraculously released.

After her release, Corrie became a tramp for the Lord. She traveled the world to share the gospel message of Jesus and his love. One time when she was speaking at a church in Munich, Germany, a man approached her at the end of the service. She recognized him as a former guard at the Ravensbruck camp.

Seeing him brought back painful memories of cruelty and of men mocking her and Betsie. The man had been one of the cruelest guards at the concentration camp but had become a Christian after the war. He thrust out his hand as he spoke. "I am grateful for your message of God's forgiveness . . . to think that Jesus washed away my sins."

Corrie prayed silently as she stood there fumbling with her pocketbook. *Jesus help me. I can lift my hand. I can do that much. You supply the feeling.* Then she took the man's hand and cried, "I forgive you, brother, with all my heart." Something amazing happened as the two shook hands. Corrie felt God's love intensely.[4] Because of the power of the Holy Spirit, she could forgive (Romans 5:5).

Saul persecuted David out of envy. He wanted to kill him at all cost and went after him with over three thousand men. When Saul went into a cave to rest, he did not know David and his men were at the back of the cave. David approached Saul while he was asleep and cut off a piece of his robe—but did not harm him (1 Samuel 24).

Because David trusted the Lord, he extended mercy to Saul. "May the Lord therefore judge which of us is right and punish the guilty one. He is my advocate, and he will rescue me from your power!" (1 Samuel 24:15 NLT).

In order to forgive, both Corrie and David had to surrender their will to God's will. Because of the power of the Holy Spirit, you and I can forgive the worst offender.

Will you ask the Holy Spirit to fill your heart with his love and power to forgive?

Prayer

Lord, there is no offense so deep
that your love cannot forgive.
Help me release those who have hurt me deeply
and trust you as my advocate.
Thank you that your love for me is deeper still.
Amen.

Intimacy with God

True Love

This is love: not that we loved God,
but that he loved us and sent his Son
as an atoning sacrifice for our sins.

1 JOHN 4:10

I would like to introduce you to my friend. He is considered the leading expert on love.

- He is the fountain of love and goodwill.
- His heart flows positively toward us at all times.
- He knows everything about everything.
- He is without distortion, without confusion, and without gaps.
- He is complete justice. His justice is based upon *all* facts and undistorted by shortfalls in emotions or knowledge.
- He is utterly faithful—to his own person, to his people, to his work.
- There is not even a hint of unfaithfulness.
- There is no shadow of turning, distraction, or relationship fatigue.
- He is sovereign; there is no power or plan higher than his.
- No law of nature, no human will or direction, no health crisis, or no marital crisis overrides his plan.
- Nothing negates his purpose.
- He is the *only* cement block upon which we can *stand* in changing circumstances.
- He is Wikipedia par excellence.
- He is the author of perfect peace, perfect joy, perfect stability, and perfect reasonableness.
- He is pure love.

I first met my friend as a young girl, but over the years have gotten to know him better. One afternoon, during a dark season in my life and marriage, I felt a presence in my van while driving to work. I started singing a song about the love of God and pulled over to the side of the road. As I sang, a deep sense of peace washed over me. I was on the roadside for a while but didn't keep track of time. Since then, I know my friend as *indescribable love*. He has helped me understand that love is an essential ingredient in all relationships.

True love is not about mushy feelings. It is a choice, a commitment, and an attitude. True love is kind, patient, and shows up every day regardless of feelings. True love sees others through the eyes of Jesus.

My friend is Jesus Christ, the Son of God who died on the cross to redeem all who believe. It is impossible to know true love without him. His love is sure, secure, and sweet.

His love brings peace and provides courage to weather any trials. His steadfast love is the glue that holds marriages and relationships together. Will you embrace his love for you?

Prayer

I am grateful for your steadfast love.
Help me to love others with your love
even when it is difficult.
With you on my side,
I can overcome the obstacles that life may bring.
Amen.

Created in Wisdom

The heavens proclaim the glory of God.
The skies display his craftsmanship.
PSALM 19:1 NLT

David faced many trials in his life, but his ability to withstand adversity can be attributed to his worship of God. Many of the psalms written by David describe the awesomeness and majesty of God and his creation.

> Lord, our Lord, how majestic is your name in all the earth!
>   You have set your glory in the heavens.
> Through the praise of children and infants you have
>   established a stronghold against your enemies, to
>   silence the foe and the avenger.
> When I consider your heavens, the work of your fingers,
>   the moon and the stars, which you have set in place,
>   what is mankind that you are mindful of them,
>   human beings that you care for them?
> You have made them a little lower than the angels
>   and crowned them with glory and honor.
> You made them rulers over the works of your hands; you
>   put everything under their feet: all flocks and herds,
>   and the animals of the wild, the birds in the sky,
>   and the fish in the sea,
>   all that swim the paths of the seas.
> Lord, our Lord, how majestic is your name in all the earth!
> (Psalm 8:1–9)

Like David, I find worship essential in overcoming my spiritual battles. My life is not perfect, and I guess yours isn't either. When we take time to reflect on God's majesty, his love, and his daily mercies toward us, we are compelled to praise him.

When I read Psalm 19, I see the futility in worrying. The words of the psalmist help me see God's hands woven through the threads of nature, my life, and my numerous trials. The Lord, our Maker, cares about us down to the smallest detail. Worship provides perspective and inspires us to choose to trust God in all situations.

Go outside at night and look at the stars. Reflect, and let what you see remind you that the God who made the stars knows you by name.

Prayer

Lord, I praise you for your beautiful
creation that reminds me you are sovereign.
Thank you for shifting my perspective
and for your guidance.
Amen.

Boundlessly Loved

Even before he made the world,
God loved us and chose us in Christ
to be holy and without fault in his eyes.

EPHESIANS 1:4 NLT

When my daughter was young, my friend used to fix her hair. Afterward, my daughter would twirl around the house and proudly announce, "Mommy, look. God made me boo'ful!" I would hug her and say, "Yes, you are very beautiful."

Our identity is a prime target for the Enemy, especially when we are facing adversity. He will constantly remind us of how we have messed up and will never measure up. Are you familiar with this voice? It brings up all kinds of negative stuff, such as: *not good enough, too fat, too skinny, not tall enough, it's your fault, if only I had* . . . (fill in the blank). This negative chatter is overwhelming.

Often, we believe the lies and allow the Enemy to define our identity. Other times, we base our worth on our jobs, accomplishments, material possessions, or status. Thankfully, there is a remedy for this identity crisis. Our identity depends on Jesus and his sacrifice on the cross. He is the true source of our identity.

Do you know who you are? If you have put your trust in Jesus and accepted him as Savior, you are a child of God. When God takes your portrait, he sees you as a beautiful woman who is:

- A crown of splendor in the Lord's hands.
- Redeemed.

- Sought after.
- No longer deserted.
- Approved.
- Dearly loved.
- Called by a new name.
- Chosen by God.

Why is it important to know our identity? In the middle of my trials, I struggled with my identity and sense of self-worth. As I searched the Scriptures, I came upon Ephesians 1:3–14 and Isaiah 62:4–12. These Scriptures became my lifeline as I meditated on them daily for over three months. As these truths penetrated my soul, I gained the courage to stand firm in faith.

Knowing and appropriating our identity in Christ is crucial to silencing the fiery lies of the Enemy and walking in victory. Reminding myself daily of my identity helped me feel grounded internally and connected with God.

Knowing our identity in Jesus enables us to stand firm in our faith.

Prayer

Lord, thank you for securing my identity in Jesus
and for loving me boundlessly.
Amen.

Soul Rest

He restores my soul.
PSALM 23:3 ESV

My friend told me about a grandfather and his granddaughter she saw while walking on the beach. The little girl, about three years old, walked ahead of him. She would stop, pick up a shell or some other interesting object and show it to her grandfather. He bent down and gently admired the object while talking to her. This happened many times as they walked unhurriedly along the beach. My friend admired the grandfather's gentleness and patience.

This story reminds me of my trips to the beach. I always look forward to going to the beach to relax. I have dealt with several challenging situations over the last ten years that often left me weary. Spending time alone on the beach in prayer helps me find soul rest and provides an opportunity to present my burdens to God.

Have you ever felt as if you were alone when carrying a heavy burden? The Lord invites us to come and find soul rest in him.

Imagine yourself sitting on the beach with a soft, cool breeze blowing in your face. You try to relax and enjoy the beautiful day, but your mind is preoccupied with your challenges, deadlines, finances, health, family, and relationship issues. You wish they would all magically disappear.

The gentle breeze beckons you to relax. You close your eyes and let go of your worries and anxieties. Immediately, the breeze feels as if it is not only on your face, but deep within your soul as a gentle, soothing massage. You hear a still, small whisper. *I love you.* Suddenly it feels as if you are in another realm. You take his hand and lean in as he draws you close in a warm embrace.

- You let go.
- You feel relaxed.
- You feel content.
- You feel refreshed.
- You hear another whisper: *I delight in you.*

The Lord loves you deeply and invites you to roll all your cares on him. He desires to restore your soul and give you rest.

Prayer

Lord, like the grandfather,
you are gentle and patient with your children.
You desire to restore my soul.
Help me exchange my burdens for your rest.
Amen.

Prayer Partners

*He urged them to ask the God of heaven
to show them his mercy by telling them the secret,
so they would not be executed
along with the other wise men of Babylon.*
DANIEL 2:18 NLT

It was 2:00 a.m. when I saw the message on my phone. I was surprised to receive a text from this former student, as I was not in regular contact with her. She sent me a Bible verse and mentioned that she woke up to pray for me and my family. Her message was timely, and the verse was like an infusion of hope in my veins. I needed that word.

Prayer is essential in navigating the storms of life, but we don't pray alone. When King Nebuchadnezzar of Babylon had a dream and none of the wise men could tell him the dream and its interpretation, he threatened to kill them. Daniel called upon three of his friends, Hananiah, Mishael, and Azariah (otherwise known as Shadrach, Meshach, and Abednego), and urged them to pray fervently that God would reveal the king's dream and its meaning. God answered their prayers and revealed the mysteries of the dream to Daniel. In return, Daniel praised and worshiped the God of heaven (Daniel 2:17–28).

Are you weathering your storm alone, or do you have others pray with you? We are not meant to weather our storms alone. We need other believers to come alongside us. I am grateful for the seasoned prayer partners who continue to support me in my storms. They are a blessing and God's ministering angels in my journey. Many times, when I face the fiery furnace of trials, I find consolation in knowing others are praying along with me.

Sometimes the Lord prompts others to pray for us who may not fully know our situation. They pray because they are intercessors who are in tune with God's Spirit.

Friend, will you allow the Lord to lighten your burden through his ministering angels? Pray and ask God to send believers to encourage you while you are in the storm.

Prayer

Lord, thank you for prayer partners
and the community of faith.
Send seasoned prayer warriors who will support me
as I walk through the storm.
Amen.

Knowing God's Will

And so, from the day we heard,
we have not ceased to pray for you,
asking that you may be filled with the knowledge of his will
in all spiritual wisdom and understanding.
COLOSSIANS 1:9 ESV

Do you know the lyrics of songs you did not intentionally memorize?

I have often found it difficult to recall Scripture from memory. One day I read an article about a woman who teaches people how to sing the Scriptures. I wondered why I had not thought of this idea. I know the lyrics to many songs by heart, but I don't remember memorizing them. By singing the Scriptures repeatedly, we remember them better. It is also a way of praying God's Word in the midst of our storms.

If you struggle to memorize and recall Scripture, singing them is a good way to pray and also get God's Word in your heart, keeping your mind sharp and in tune with God's will. In Old Testament times, the Israelites sang many of the psalms in prayer and praise to God. Praying to know God's will about our situation will help us gain God's perspective. Often, our understanding of God's purpose for our difficulties is limited. When we gain his perspective, we have peace.

Paul prayed for the Colossians to have knowledge of God's will so they would know and understand what God was doing and live fulfilled lives. This practice of hiding God's Word in my heart has helped me to pray better, especially knowing I can pray God's words when I don't have words of my own.

Knowing and understanding God's will connects us with the heart of God for our situation.

Prayer

Long ago, David and the Israelites sang the psalms.
Thank you for showing me that I can sing your Word.
I invite you to write your Word on my heart
so I may gain a deeper understanding
of where you are working in my situation.
Grant me peace as I lean on your unfailing love.
Amen.

My Place of Safety

But I will sing about your strength.
In the morning I will sing about your love.
You are my defender, my place of safety
in times of trouble.
PSALM 59:16 NCV

Do you like singing? I don't have a good singing voice, but I love to make a joyful noise to the Lord. During the fiercest battles for my marriage, my children's health, and family finances, I was often weary and had no words. During these low moments, a song or two would come into my heart. As I sang, the weariness would lift.

Paul and Silas found themselves imprisoned. The situation was dire. Rather than complain, they prayed and praised the Lord while the other prisoners were listening. They recognized that God alone was their place of safety. While singing, the Lord came as a mighty deliverer, and a violent earthquake shook the foundations of the prison. The doors flew open. All the prisoners' chains fell off, including Paul's and Silas's (Acts 16:25–26).

It took an act of faith for Paul and Silas to remember God as their strength and the only place of safety while they were in prison. Though they did not understand how God would deliver them, their actions reflected their trust in him.

Where is your place of strength and safety when trouble comes? What chains and prison are you dealing with today?

As we look to the Lord and lean on his strength through prayer and praise, we can trust our prison doors to open and our chains to fall off. When my family faced various challenges, I ran to the Lord and looked to him as my place of safety. Singing about God's love reinforced my faith. God brought my family through it all.

Praise your way through your chains and watch them fall off in Jesus's name. May you be encouraged to trust God and know he can break every chain and deliver you from every struggle, including heartaches, health issues, finances, and loneliness.

Prayer

Lord, I am encouraged that when I am
bombarded by the storms of life,
you are a place of safety I can run to.
I trust you to deliver me
and bring good out of seemingly terrible situations.
Fill my heart with songs of praise and worship.
Amen.

Unwavering Trust

Those who live in the shelter of the Most High
will find rest in the shadow of the Almighty.
This I declare about the Lord:
He alone is my refuge, my place of safety;
he is my God, and I trust him.

PSALM 91:1-2 NLT

Can you remember a time when you had to make a difficult choice?

I was once a leader in a Bible study, and the leaders met at 5:00 a.m. once a week to discuss the lesson for the following week. I faced a serious family situation and prayed through the night about it. I was torn between staying home to keep an eye on the situation or trusting God by going to the leaders' meeting. After more prayer and talking with God, I took God at his Word and went to the meeting.

I recognized the situation was no longer about me. It was about my faith. Did I trust that God was big enough to handle this situation?

Psalm 91:1-2 describes an intimate relationship between two people. After all, you don't hide in someone's shadow if you have no connection with them. These verses paint a picture of a trusting, loving, and dependent relationship where David saw God as his refuge, security, close confidant, and someone he could depend on at any time. He acknowledged God's supremacy and control over all as he declared his unwavering faith that God is who he says he is.

While driving, I meditated on these verses and asked God to

help me apply these truths to my current situation. I shared with the other leaders, and together, all fifty of us lifted our voices in prayer. After the meeting, I went home to find the tense situation resolved. My fears never materialized. This experience taught me and the other leaders what it looks like to have unwavering trust in God.

When the rubber meets the road and you face difficult circumstances, what is your response? Do you trust God to handle any situation? No matter the challenges you are facing, be encouraged. God is faithful and worthy of your trust. You can hide under the shadow of his wings.

Prayer

Father, thank you for your amazing grace and love.
Thank you for providing me
with a place of rest, shelter, and security in you
when life is hard.
Help me trust you daily.
Amen.

Leave Your Native Country

The Lord had said to Abram,
"Leave your native country,
your relatives, and your father's family,
and go to the land that I will show you."
GENESIS 12:1 NLT

When I left my home country to come to the United States, I was not sure what to expect. There were a lot of unknowns. I would be far from home and my parents. The only person I knew was my husband. I was anxious about moving.

In Genesis 12, God called Abram to leave his homeland for a land that he would show him. God promised Abram he would make him into a great nation and that all the peoples of the earth would be blessed through him. Abram obeyed the Lord and moved to a new land.

Our trials provide opportunities to go on an adventure with the Lord. They often require us to leave the old, familiar country and move to a new country. Abram's relocation is a metaphor for our life's journey. When we accept Jesus Christ as Lord and Savior, we are commanded to leave our old life, which is our native country. In the native country, we are comfortable and indulge in fleshly desires, but it takes time to leave the old behind. Often it is only during trials and challenges that we consider making the needed changes.

Moving to the new country is a spiritual relocation rather than a physical relocation. Our trials provide opportunities to have an inner renewal in the spirit, where our desires, core beliefs, attitudes, and thoughts are renewed and better aligned to be more Christlike. Leaving my native land for the promised land helps me put off my old way of living and put on the new way of living so I can grow in the image of Christ (2 Corinthians 5:17; Ephesians 4:22–24).

Spiritual relocation is a calling to experience deeper intimacy with God, be filled with the Holy Spirit, and live an abundant life. Are you ready to go on an adventure with God? Ask him to help you move today.

Prayer

Father, thank you for sending your son
to die on the cross for my sins.
Help me leave my old, familiar country
with all its comforts
and come on this adventure with you
so I can experience the best life you have for me.
I ask in Jesus's precious name.
Amen.

Firm Foundation

When a flood came, the torrent struck that house
but could not shake it because it was well built.
LUKE 6:48

During our mission trip in Ethiopia, we traveled to a rural a village to minister to women. Throughout the trip, there was a heavy downpour. As we got to the outskirts of the village, we couldn't go farther, because the bridge on the only road was washed out. We waited for a while to figure out the best way to cross the river without sinking our vehicle.

Why was the bridge washed out? Because of its weak foundation. Our lives are like the bridge. Without a firm foundation, we will collapse and fall apart when the storms of life hit. Jesus used this story to illustrate the similarity between hearing his Word and practicing it. Everyone who hears God's Word and applies it is like a wise person who builds their house on a firm foundation. When the storms of life hit and they face multiple challenges, they will not be shaken because their foundation is built on Christ—the solid rock.

What foundation is your house built on? Will it withstand the storms of life? Weathering our storms well depends on our foundation. When we face the torrents of life's rain lashing against us as pain, disappointment, betrayal, or financial loss, we can stand firm if our foundation is built on Christ, because we have a personal relationship with him and we trust him. He is always ready to provide the support we need.

As I look back on my life, I honestly do not know how I could have withstood the multitude of challenges my family faced one after another without a solid relationship with Jesus. In 2015 alone, we faced job loss, severe health crises, and a house fire, which left us homeless. When the storms came, we leaned heavily on Jesus. He is our anchor and hope in the storm.

Prayer

Lord, I want to build my house on your solid rock. Help me cultivate
a deeper relationship with you
so I can trust you with my challenges.
Guide me and give me wisdom each day.
Amen.

What Is True about God?

Our Father in heaven, hallowed be your name.
MATTHEW 6:9 ESV

Can I let you in on a secret?

Reminding myself of who God is has been one of the greatest things to help me stand during some of the fiercest battles the Enemy waged against my family. It was during a crisis that I wrote the attributes of God in a notebook and prayed them aloud regularly.

There is nothing like worship to soothe the weary soul. When we recognize God for who he is and worship him, we will experience a peace beyond our understanding. In my experience, worship is an essential ingredient in fighting for your life, family, marriage, and anything dear to you. Worship will silence the Enemy, energize you, and release the supernatural power of God. It helps shift your focus and reminds you who is in control.

Reflecting on what I know to be true about God anchors my heart to his heart. It brings me to a place of quiet rest in him and shifts my perspective from my circumstances to God.

What do you know to be true about God, and how will you let his truths soothe your soul? Let's worship him together, shall we?

Our Father, we honor your name.
You are the Most High God and the King of kings.
You heal the brokenhearted and bind up their wounds.
You number the stars and call them by name.

O Lord, you are great and mighty in power.
Your understanding has no limit.
You are the Rock of Ages and the Ancient of Days.
You are the Author of life; besides you there is no other.
You are the Lion of the tribe of Judah;
Everlasting Father and Omnipotent God.
The Restorer of broken ruins.
The Source of hope.
You are gracious and full of compassion.
My Righteousness and Redeemer.
You reached down from on high and took hold of me.
You drew me out of deep waters.
O Lord, my God, how majestic is your name in all the earth.
You alone are worthy of my praise.

Prayer

Father, thank you for being the Lord of my life.
I will trust in your name forever.
Amen.

One Thing

There is only one thing
worth being concerned about.
Mary has discovered it,
and it will not be taken away from her.
LUKE 10:42 NLT

When my children were younger, we celebrated their birthdays with their friends in our home. As I planned the celebrations, I created to-do lists to guide my preparations. My plans included sending out invitations, cleaning and decorating the house, shopping for food items and party favors, cooking, and baking the cake. Many times I found that my to-do lists left me feeling overwhelmed.

Martha was the queen of hospitality. She and her sister, Mary, were hosting Jesus and his disciples in their home. While Martha loved entertaining, she did not have time to sit and enjoy the company of her guests, because there was still a lot to do.

On the other hand, Mary sat and listened to Jesus's teaching. In frustration, Martha asked Jesus to tell Mary to help her. Jesus replied that Mary's choice of the *one thing worth being concerned about* would not be taken from her.

I can relate to Martha's feelings of being stressed. Our constant busyness often makes us lose sight of what is most important. I remember days when I did not have enough time to sit and relax. I mostly prayed on the run. But when I landed on hard times, I was forced to reevaluate my priorities and align them with the most important thing . . . the thing that Mary chose.

Spending time with God in his Word and cultivating a life of prayer and worship are vital to weathering the storms of life. Sitting and soaking in the presence of Jesus is the *one thing* that is essential to experiencing His power.

What is keeping you from experiencing this *one thing*?

Prayer

Lord, sometimes I neglect
spending quality time with you
and worry over things that are not as important.
Help me reduce the distractions in my life
so I can experience your presence, joy, and peace with a grateful heart.
Amen.

Take a Risk

Lord, if it is really you,
tell me to come to you walking on the water.
MATTHEW 14:28 NLT

In 2012, I took a risk and went on my first mission trip for two and a half weeks in rural Ethiopia. I left my normal routine to share the love of Jesus with women. Going on a mission trip was not on my radar, but the trip stretched me and grew my faith.

Imagine leaving the comfort of home in the United States, where you have constant internet access, phone, email, and instant meals, in exchange for sleeping on the hard mud ground, dry baths with baby wipes, bugs, and amazing people.

Jesus and the disciples had just finished feeding a large crowd of over five thousand people. It was a long day of ministry, so the disciples were glad when Jesus asked them to get in the boat and cross to the other side of the lake. They were far from the shore when they encountered strong winds and waves that threatened to overturn the boat. Then they saw someone walking toward them on the water. They were terrified.

But then Jesus spoke to them to calm their fears. "'Don't be afraid,' he said. 'Take courage. I am here'" (Matthew 14:27 NLT). Peter asked Jesus to call him to come. He stepped out of the boat and walked on water toward Jesus, but when he saw the strong waves, he was afraid and started to sink. Peter took a risk that stretched his faith.

Jesus used that situation to strengthen the disciples' faith, just as he used the mission trip to Ethiopia to increase my faith. I saw women shed tears of joy as they embraced their identity in Christ and his love for them. As I allowed God to take control of my trials, I began to see my challenges as opportunities to take risks for him and grow in my faith and character.

Growing in faith requires taking a risk. No matter your situation, God can use what you see as a difficulty to grow your faith.

What risks are you willing to take that God can use to increase your faith?

Prayer

Lord, help me to see risk-taking
from your perspective.
Thank you that you desire to increase my faith
and grow my character through my life's events.
Amen.

Inner Strength

I pray that from his glorious, unlimited resources
he will empower you with inner strength through his Spirit.
EPHESIANS 3:16 NLT

A few years ago, I was thirty pounds overweight. I realized that losing weight meant I had to make changes. I struggled initially to determine the plan of action, but I decided that losing weight required effort and being intentional. My plan was simple. Every night before going to bed, I had a talk with myself as I laid out my exercise clothes and shoes.

It took time to be consistent, but twelve years later I am still working this plan. I have gained physical and spiritual strength, as I now view my exercise time as a way to connect with God in prayer.

In our spiritual life, we may be out of shape and need to "lose a few pounds." Paul's prayer for the Ephesians (Ephesians 1:16–19 NLT) is a great prayer to own as we seek inner strength to grow in wisdom and knowledge.

> I have not stopped thanking God for you. I pray for you consistently, asking God, the glorious Father of our Lord Jesus Christ, to give you spiritual wisdom and insight so that you might grow in your knowledge of God. I pray that your hearts will be flooded with light so that you can understand the confident hope he has given to those he called—his holy people who are his rich and glorious inheritance. I also pray that you will understand the incredible greatness of God's power for us who believe him.

Paul's prayer helps me to better align my prayers with God's heart. Often, when I think about my struggles, I want relief. But God's plans rarely lead to an immediate answer. That's when I must learn to endure, because "endurance produces character, and character produces hope" (Romans 5:4 ESV). Cultivating inner strength builds our resilience, perseverance, and character.

What weights are you willing to shed to gain God's inner strength? Personalize Paul's prayer and ask God to help you.

Prayer

Lord, I praise you for the privileges I have in you.
Help me tap into your unlimited resources
to gain inner strength and wisdom
to pursue your purpose for my life.
Thank you for using the very things I kick against
to teach me patience, compassion, love, empathy,
and speaking the truth in love.
Thank you for instructing me in the way of wisdom
and guiding me on a straight path.
Amen.

Raging Storm

The Lord is gracious and righteous;
our God is full of compassion.
PSALM 116:5

Lord, it is me
On this dark night
Alone on a lonely country road
I look in the rearview mirror
There is no other car
All around me is a raging storm
Loud roar and peals of thunder
Flashes of lightning
Showcase a generous display
of your majesty in the night sky
I try to focus on the road ahead
But my thoughts consume me
The storm raging outside
Is a mirror of my life
Heavy downpour
Hard to see the road
But a few feet at a time
Lord, how am I ever going
to come out of this storm?
This thought stays for a while
I lean forward for a better view of the road
Then in a gentle whisper

I hear
One step at a time
Just like you are doing right now
The storm will rage
At times it will be too fierce
And almost knock you out
But keep your eyes on me
I will guide you
Do not be afraid.

Prayer

From a deep, dark pit,
hopelessness swirls all around me
and the darkness threatens to engulf me.
I cry to you for help.
Because of your compassion, mercy, and unfailing love,
Lord, you hear my cry and you rescue me.
Thank you for never forsaking me
when the storm is raging all around me.
Thank you that nothing can separate me
from your love.
I bless you, Lord.
Amen.

Be Anxious for Nothing

Do not be anxious about anything
but in every situation by prayer and petition with thanksgiving,
present your request to God.
And the peace of God which transcends all understanding
will guard your hearts and your minds
in Christ Jesus.

PHILIPPIANS 4:6–7

We had just returned home from grocery shopping. The kids got out of the car, and as my son ran up the steps, he fell. The bottle he was holding broke and cut him deeply. My mama heart skipped a few beats as blood gushed from his wrist. I found a scarf, tied it around his wrist to stop the bleeding, and rushed him to the emergency room.

While driving, I tried to still my thoughts, but it was difficult as all kinds of questions filled my mind. *Will they be able to repair his wrist? What if they can't fix it? What will we do?* At some point, I stopped myself and turned to prayer. I asked the Lord to go before us and guide the doctors on how to best take care of my son.

By the time we arrived at the emergency room, my son was calm and I had peace.

What are you anxious about today? Instead of worry, pray. You have a Father in heaven who loves you beyond measure and desires to calm your anxious heart. He wants you to depend on him. As you do, he will give you unexplainable peace that will guard your mind.

When something on your mind fills you with anxiety, bring it to the Lord in prayer and tell him, "Lord, I cast this problem upon you." Whenever the anxious thought sneaks back into your mind, say out loud, "This problem belongs to Jesus. I already gave it to him." Do this and see how the Lord takes care of each of your worries.

This is the best way I have found to cast my cares on the Lord and to guard my heart. When the Enemy wants to steal my peace, I remind myself that I have God's peace as long as I keep my mind on him (Isaiah 26:3). Fixing my mind on God and his Word keeps me in God's supernatural peace.

Prayer

Lord, your peace is a promise
that is available to all who trust you
and cast their cares on you.
Thank you for filling me with your peace.
I praise you, Lord, for the gift of your peace.
Amen.

Divine Intercession

In the same way, the Spirit helps us in our weakness.
We do not know what we ought to pray for,
but the Spirit himself intercedes for us
through wordless groans.
ROMANS 8:26

As a twenty-something-year-old, I was confident. I had ideas for what my life would look like and set out to work on my goals. I was driven, goal-oriented, and focused on whatever task needed to be completed. This wasn't bad except that I primarily ran in my own strength. Though I knew the Lord and prayed often, his words did not influence the way I lived my life.

Fast-forward twenty-four years later. I was out of steam. Life had involuntarily enrolled me in the school of hard knocks. My life looked bleak as I stared down the pit of depression and hopelessness. What happened? I had many questions but few answers.

During that season of my life, all I wanted to do was lie in bed and feel sorry for myself. I couldn't pray. I knew a lot of Scripture, but it was no use. There were no words. It was as if someone erased the hard drive. I felt empty. Abandoned. Done.

But during my despair, Jesus was there. He never left. When I had no words, he had groans. He didn't need words. Groans were just enough for the moment. His Spirit interceded for me. He pleaded with the Father for mercy, for grace, for strength, and for renewal. As my advocate, he was relentless to bring me back to life in him.

Then he worked tirelessly to heal my soul wounds and realign my priorities with his will and purpose for my life. One day I noticed an increased desire to read and meditate on God's Word. As I did, the words came alive and popped off the page. He replaced my soul bareness with his love, obedience, empathy, and forgiveness. I was once again abiding in him.

God desires to work on your behalf. He is patient, gracious, and merciful. Whatever issues you may be dealing with, you don't have to wait until you reach the end of your rope. Look up—he is reaching out to you. Will you take his outstretched arms and let him help you?

Prayer

Father, when I thought I knew best,
you showed me how little I knew of myself.
You took me and introduced me to your love.
Thank you for reaching out to me
and making me so much better.
Amen.

Fasting and Prayer

This kind can come out only by prayer.
MARK 9:29

I grew up in a home where fasting and prayers were a part of our spiritual practice. As a child, I would fast till about noon, and then my parents would pray with me. They taught me to read Scriptures and memorize them during this time. Fasting provided my parents opportunities to seek spiritual guidance for important decisions such as when we were going back to boarding school, relocation, job changes, or when relatives were coming to live with us.

It is only in the last few years I have come to appreciate the benefits of fasting and prayer in enhancing my relationship with God. Fasting is abstaining from food, water, or other pleasures for a spiritual purpose.

Why should believers fast?

The Bible includes several accounts of fasting and prayer. In Mark 9, when the disciples encountered a boy who was demon possessed, they could not drive out the demon. Later, in private, the disciples asked Jesus why they couldn't drive out the demon. Jesus responded, "This kind cannot be driven out by anything but prayer and fasting" (Mark 9:29 AMPC).

Esther called the Jews to fast for three days while she prepared to go to the king on their behalf (Esther 4:16). Daniel fasted regularly. Jesus fasted forty days and forty nights and resisted temptation (Matthew 4:1–4). The prophetess Anna worshiped God with prayer and fasting (Luke 2:36–37).

Though there is no hard rule about fasting, there are various reasons to embrace this discipline. I would not have survived the enormous spiritual warfare I've experienced since 2007 without fasting and prayer. This is an essential tool if you want to intercede for others and engage in spiritual warfare.

When should a believer fast? I encourage you to study the following reasons:

- Need for urgent prayer. (1 Kings 21:27–29; Psalm 35:13)
- Spiritual development and deeper fellowship with God. (Exodus 24:18)
- Interceding for God's people. (Deuteronomy 9:8–9; Ezra 10:6)
- Ordination of elders and commissioning. (Acts 13:3; Acts 14:23)
- Repentance from sin. (Nehemiah 9:1–3; Joel 1:14; Jonah 3:5–10)
- To build up your prayer life and confidence in God. (Daniel 9:7–11, 20–23; Matthew 6:9–13)
- Spiritual cleansing and insights. (Acts 9:17–18)
- Spiritual deliverance. (2 Chronicles 20:3–4, 29; Isaiah 58:6)
- Self-discipline. (Daniel 10:2–3; Isaiah 58:3; Exodus 16:49)
- Direction. (Judges 20:26–28; Ezra 8:21–23; Acts 13:2–3)

Our motives for fasting must be pure and come from a joyful attitude, not to show off or brag, like hypocrites (Luke 18:9–14).

Prayer

Lord, thank you for the gifts
of worship, praise, prayer, and fasting
as elements to increase our faith
and help us experience your supernatural power
in greater depth.
Amen.

Tuned In

O Lord, do good to those who are good,
whose hearts are in tune with you.

PSALM 125:4 NLT

One way I tune in to God is through regular ongoing prayer. It is my declaration of dependence on God.

One Sunday as I got ready for church, I heard in my spirit, *Pray over your daughter before she leaves home this morning.* I made a note to pray with her later.

As I prepared for church, we were running late. I almost forgot but stopped and prayed over my daughter as I felt prompted. I prayed for protection during her soccer game later in the day. After church, I went to watch her game. I had been there less than five minutes when another player collided with my daughter and knocked her unconscious.

I ran to the scene. My heart was racing. *O Lord, please help her be okay. Thank you for prompting me to pray for her this morning.* While the officials attended to her, I sent out prayer requests to my prayer groups.

The Lord kept my daughter, but she suffered a concussion that changed the course of our lives. If you are a mom, you know the anguish mothers experience when their children face traumatic experiences.

This incident has had the most impact on stretching my faith and dependence on God. It has not been an easy walk. Rather, it has taken me to the end of myself and back. It has caused me to understand surrender on a new level. For the first time, I understand what Abraham must have felt when he offered Isaac up as a sacrifice (Genesis 22:9–12).

It has caused me to tune my heart in and say, *Lord, your will be done.*

What life experience has had the most impact on you and helped you tune in more to the Lord?

Prayer

Lord, you are my hiding place.
Your everlasting arms uphold me
and protect me from trouble.
You surround me with songs of victory.
I rest in your unfailing love.
Amen.

Broken into Beautiful

For I am not ashamed of the gospel,
because it is the power of God
that brings salvation to everyone who believes.
ROMANS 1:16

What is the point of suffering? I did not always comprehend the full purpose until I experienced major life challenges. As I wrestled with suffering as part of life, I came to a new realization. Rather than ask *why*, I shifted my thoughts to *what*.

God, what is your purpose in this situation? Give me your viewpoint. Reframing my questions to *what* unfolded new perspectives. I see now it is about purpose and growing in character. It is about sharing in the fellowship of Jesus's suffering and conforming to the image of Christ (Philippians 3:10).

Viewed from this perspective, suffering takes on a new meaning. Our sufferings and brokenness are not to be avoided but embraced. "Instead, be very glad—for these trials make you partners with Christ in his suffering, so that you will have the wonderful joy of seeing his glory when it is revealed to all the world" (1 Peter 4:13 NLT).

Suffering prepares us to partake with others in their brokenness and share the good news of Jesus wherever we go, whether it is at work, in our neighborhoods, or at the grocery store. There is a greater purpose in our brokenness.

Many in our society are facing hopelessness. The suicide rate is at an all-time high and does not discriminate, as it affects all ages—

men, women, and children.

Having experienced the life-giving hope of Jesus in my brokenness, I am here to give you hope. You are chosen and loved. Your suffering is a part of God's bigger picture for your life. One day you will look back and see your brokenness turn into beauty. Embrace the purpose in your pain. If your story touches and transforms one person's life, it is well worth it.

What blessings have you experienced in your brokenness? Who can you encourage today?

Prayer

Suffering is a great teacher.
Like a mirror, it forces me to stop
and take a second look at myself.
Lord, thank you for helping me see my brokenness
through the eyes of eternity.
Amen.

Time Alone with God

*The earnest prayer of a righteous person
has great power and produces wonderful results.*
JAMES 5:16 NLT

For years I struggled with praying in English because, growing up, I learned to pray in my native language of Yoruba. The Yoruba phrases don't always have parallels in English. When I moved to America, I had to get over my fear of praying aloud in English. I learned by praying every morning alone in my bedroom.

The secret to a victorious life is spending time alone with God in prayer daily. Jesus fought his greatest battles in prayer. He went away often and alone to a quiet place to talk to his Father. Before he was arrested and crucified, he went with his disciples to a place called Gethsemane, and he said to them, "Sit here while I go over there and pray. . . . My soul is overwhelmed with sorrow to the point of death; stay here and keep watch with me" (Matthew 26:36, 38).

If Jesus, the Son of God, can make time to be alone with God, we have no reason not to follow his example. Although other people can pray for us, it is not a substitute for having a heart-to-heart connection with God through regular prayer.

It was through dealing with my frustrations, disappointments, and family crises I got a better handle on praying in English. I have no formula. During my prayer time, I have an honest conversation with the Lord about what is on my heart, and I find out what is on his heart as I listen for his voice. Don't worry about presenting a perfect prayer. Simply talk to God as you would a friend.

Regular prayer doesn't have to be legalistic or a chore we check off our list. It is a commitment to constant communication with the Lord throughout the day (1 Thessalonians 5:17). If you are too busy to talk to God, then you cannot expect to grow in your relationship with him. It requires time. Growing your prayer life will make you worry less and increase your sensitivity to the Holy Spirit. It will also boost your confidence that God hears you. "Don't worry about anything; instead, pray about everything. Tell God what you need and thank him for all he has done" (Philippians 4:6 NLT).

What is the need of your heart today? Tell God about it and keep track of your requests in a journal. In time you will marvel at how God answers.

If you desire to weather storms well, you need to cultivate a life of prayer. This is best learned by doing.

Prayer

Lord, I desire to spend time with you alone
to strengthen my relationship with you.
Thank you for giving me confidence
to ask for anything
and for answering my prayers
according to your will.
Amen.

Sons and Daughters of the King

Then Gideon asked Zebah and Zalmunna,
"The men you killed at Tabor—what were they like?"
"Like you," they replied. "They all had the look of a king's son."
JUDGES 8:18 NLT

What does a king's son or daughter look like?

Gideon went after the Midianites—who were terrorizing Israel—and captured the two kings who had killed his brothers at Tabor. He asked them, "The men you killed, what did they look like?"

The Midianite kings responded, "They all had the look of a king's son."

The response of the Midianite kings caused me to reflect on my identity and what a prince or princess looks like. Sadly, many of us don't know or fully embrace our status as royalty and children of God. If the Enemy knows our status as sons and daughters of the King, why do we not know or embrace it ourselves?

We don't know our identity because, most times, we allow our circumstances to define us. The truth is, God loves us and knows every intricate detail of our lives. He does not define us by our challenges. Psalm 139 paints an excellent portrait of how God sees you and me. He knew us when we were intricately woven in our mother's womb, fearfully and wonderfully made, and God's hand of blessing is on our heads.

As a son or daughter of the King, you are born of imperishable seed. You are the apple of the King's eyes, eternally redeemed, and completely forgiven. He ordains every moment of your life. You are righteous, blameless, and seated in heavenly places.

His thoughts toward you are good. You are hidden in Christ and eternally secure. You are bold, more than a conqueror, and the sweet smell of Jesus to those who are perishing. As a child of God, you are like a tree planted by the water that bears fruit in season. Best of all, you are the son or daughter whom Jesus loves.

Friend, embrace your identity. You are royalty, a daughter or son of the King.

Prayer

Lord, forgive me for my ignorance.
Thank you for my salvation
and all the perks that come with being royalty.
Help me see, feel, know, and walk
in my identity in Christ.
Wherever I go,
let your glory be revealed in my life.
I love you, Lord.
Amen.

Glory Revealed

There he was transfigured before them.
His face shone like the sun,
and his clothes became as white as light.
MATTHEW 17:2

Driving home from Bible study one night, the Lord brought a young man to mind. I quieted my spirit to discern what the Lord wanted me to do. I sensed the young man was in some kind of trouble, so I prayed for him in the car and most of the night. The next day, I got a text from his mom requesting prayer for him.

I am humbled that God would reveal himself to a broken woman like me and invite me to partner with his work in another person's life. One benefit of adversity and storms is that God reveals his glory to us in a deeper way.

Jesus took John, James, and Peter—the three men in his inner circle—up to the mountain to pray. There the men witnessed Jesus transformed into his full glory as his face shone and his clothes turned bright as light. Then Elijah and Moses appeared. While Jesus was talking with them, God affirmed Jesus as his beloved Son. "This is my Son whom I love. Listen to him!" (Mark 9:7).

If Peter, James, and John had any doubts about the identity of Jesus, this experience cemented it for them to recognize Jesus as the Messiah. In a similar way, suffering and adversity can shine God's light on our heart and help us evaluate our beliefs. The result is a deeper awareness of God and his workings around us.

As we draw closer to God in our trials, he will reveal himself to us in ways beyond our imagination. We develop increased sensitivity to the ways he communicates with us, which could be through the Scriptures, dreams, or promptings in our spirit. He also produces good fruits such as patience, kindness, love, and humility in us.

Through my trials, I am growing closer to God. I am more sensitive to the Holy Spirit's promptings. The joy of every believer is to behold the glory and beauty of Jesus, to walk in his light, and to become a messenger of hope. If it takes suffering to get that, I welcome it.

How will you allow Jesus to transform you in your trials so he can reveal his glory to you?

Prayer

Lord, my suffering is real and personal,
but I know you can use it to produce good fruit in me.
Help me to be open to your Spirit,
and use me as a messenger
to bring your hope to others.
Thank you for showing me your glory.
I bless your name.
Amen.

Walk in the Spirit

Since we live by the Spirit, let us keep in step with the Spirit.
GALATIANS 5:25

When I was growing up, we ate three times a day with no snacks in between. For many years, my devotional life followed a similar pattern—comprised of one quick devotion in the morning with no check-ins with the Lord during the day.

It took a major crisis before I recognized that my devotional practice was not meeting my needs. I was unfulfilled spiritually. In Galatians 5:25, Paul tells us what we need in order to live a fulfilled life. He encourages us to walk in the Spirit, to be led by the Spirit, and to keep in step with the Spirit.

How do we walk in the Spirit? By allowing the Holy Spirit to have full access. By giving him full control of our lives. It means we are in constant communication with God throughout the day.

For me, keeping in step with the Holy Spirit involves allowing my life to be in sync and tuning my spiritual antenna in to him. It is living by the power of the Holy Spirit 24/7, listening for his promptings, and praying in the Spirit with thanksgiving wherever I am, whether at work, driving, cooking, or on my morning walk. I ask the Lord to provide opportunities to serve him throughout the day. I ask him to show me who needs a phone call, text, prayer, or encouragement. Though I am still a work in progress, being led by the Spirit makes me feel like I am talking with my best friend.

Walking in the Spirit is a continuous process of surrendering and yielding control to Jesus. Keeping in step with the Spirit will deepen our relationship with God, fill our spiritual tanks, and help us see our storms through God's lens. If we rely on anything besides the Holy Spirit, we will run into trouble. Jesus told Peter to watch and pray so he would not fall into temptation. Peter did not keep in step with the Spirit, so he fell and denied Jesus three times (Matthew 26:41).

Keeping in step with the Spirit is essential to weathering life's storms well and staying out of the devil's snares. As we allow the Holy Spirit to control our lives and conduct, the Lord will lead us.

God has a great plan and purpose for you. Are you relying on anything other than the Holy Spirit for help?

Prayer

Father, I am willing to walk in the Spirit,
but many times I fall short.
Holy Spirit, help me.
Fill me with yourself.
Let my steps be in sync with you;
I want to be led by you.
Thank you, Lord.
Amen.

Hope in the Storm

Look Up

I look up to the mountains—does my help come from there?
PSALM 121:1 NLT

"Mom! Wake up! The house is on fire."

I opened my eyes slowly, thinking I was dreaming. To my surprise, my daughter was standing in the doorway of my bedroom, urgently calling me. "Mom, get up! We have to get out now. The house is on fire!"

By the time I got up, the house was filling with smoke. We barely made it out in time.

Flames billowed from the roof at the back of the house. Fortunately, someone had called 911. There were nine fire trucks on the street, and firefighters rushed around the house trying to put out the flames. As we stood on the street, I watched in disbelief. Many thoughts and questions bombarded my mind. *Why? Have we not suffered enough? When will all this suffering end?*

When we are in the middle of a storm, it is difficult to see clearly. We often look at the problem and feel completely overwhelmed. But God reminds us that he is in control even when we cannot feel or sense him. As we stood outside watching the firefighters, I looked up to the sky, and there was the moon shining ever so brightly. The words *I look up to the mountains* came to mind. Knowing this was where my help would come from, I prayed silently. I told God I didn't understand how we would make it through this crisis, but I thanked him in advance for how he would help us.

God answered our prayers, as friends and family rallied around to support us in our time of crisis. Looking back, my family's help came from the Lord. He provided in ways beyond our imagination. A family allowed us to stay in their rental unit free of charge until our house was rebuilt.

Perhaps you are experiencing an unexpected storm. If so, may I encourage you to look up! The Lord, the Creator of heaven and earth, is on your side and is with you in your storm.

Prayer

Lord, help me look up to you
during challenging times.
Thank you for your ever-present help in times of trouble.
Thank you for your provision and protection.
Amen.

Joy in the Storms

Even though I walk
through the valley of the shadow of death,
I will fear no evil, for you are with me.

PSALM 23:4 ESV

My friend Becky knew a thing or two about storms. Looking at her, you would never guess she was battling an aggressive disease. She grew up as a missionary kid in Ethiopia and, from a young age, had a heart for missions. In her fifties, she returned to Ethiopia to share the gospel.

While fulfilling her new calling, Becky encountered a major storm. She was diagnosed with advanced cancer. She was determined to continue her ministry activities in Ethiopia, but as her cancer progressed, it became impossible for her to travel. Becky decided that if she could not go, she would stay back and organize volunteers to go to Ethiopia and spread the gospel. She was determined that cancer would not deter her passion for sharing her love for Jesus.

Becky modeled what it means to live in the valley of the shadow of death and fear no evil. Her passion for God was contagious. I often wondered how she could have such joy given her cancer diagnosis and the rigorous treatment. Becky's joy flowed out of a deep, loving relationship with her heavenly Father.

Job had a personal 911 crisis that left him devastated. As he received one bad piece of news after another, life bottomed out. Everything looked bleak. He lost his children, livestock, wealth, and everything he owned in one day (see Job 1). It looked as if all hope was gone. Even his wife asked him to curse God and die. Can you imagine losing your children and all you owned in one day?

What sustained Becky and Job when they found themselves in dark, desperate situations? Long before their adversity, they both set their hearts on developing a relationship with God. The book of Job provides an excellent account of how Job weathered his storm. We don't need to wait until we are in the valley before we cry out to the Lord.

Knowing Jesus and developing an intimate relationship with him before encountering storms will help us weather them well.

In what ways will you trust God to walk with you through your valley?

Prayer

Lord, sometimes my trials
can feel overwhelming,
but you promise to walk with me
through each one.
I need your strength, joy, and peace today.
Amen.

Do Not Be Afraid

So don't be afraid;
you are worth more than many sparrows.
MATTHEW 10:31

Do you sometimes worry?

Trials open the door to worry, doubt, and anxiety. Although I have been journaling privately for many years, I was anxious about sharing my writing publicly. I worried that I might interpret the Scriptures incorrectly. As such, I spent hours researching, writing, and revising to ensure my writing was good enough.

Before Jesus sent the twelve disciples into the surrounding villages to preach the gospel, he addressed many of their concerns. He reminded them not to be afraid, because they were more valuable than sparrows. These tiny birds were so common, they were cheap. If God does not forget tiny sparrows, surely the disciples could trust him to care for them too. "Are not two sparrows sold for a penny? Yet not one of them will fall to the ground outside your Father's care" (Matthew 10:29).

When we step out to do what God has called us to do, we may feel overwhelmed by fear, worry, and anxiety. This is understandable, but at some point, we need to believe our performance, accomplishments, successes, or failures do not define us.

Eventually, I let go of my worries about writing. I chose to believe God and step out in faith. Each time I sit down to write, I pray and ask the Holy Spirit to inscribe the message on my heart and transfer it to my fingers as I type. Through many trials, God has faithfully enabled me to blog for the past five years.

The sparrow is a small bird. It never has to worry about life's challenges. God is faithful and committed to meeting his children's needs beyond their wildest imagination. If he can provide for the sparrows, you can trust him with your needs. He knows the number of hairs on your head (Matthew 10:30).

Prayer

Lord, I confess my worries and anxieties,
especially when I face
uncertain and stressful situations.
Grant me the wisdom
to let go of fear
and trust you every day.
Amen.

New Beginnings

O Sovereign Lord!
You made the heavens and earth
by your strong hand and powerful arm.
Nothing is too hard for you!
JEREMIAH 32:17 NLT

As a young twenty-something-year-old, moving to the United States marked new beginnings for me and my husband. While I was excited about making new friends and learning about another culture, I experienced a lot of anxiety about the unknown.

Besides my husband, I had no friends. I anticipated being lonely and disconnected as I worried about being separated from my parents and siblings.

The children of Israel faced a lot of uncertainties with the threat of invasion by the Babylonian army. Yet God instructed the prophet Jeremiah to buy land and store the deed of purchase in a clay jar. Jeremiah took a step of faith and believed they would buy houses, fields, and vineyards again in the future, just as the Lord told him (Jeremiah 32:8–15). After purchasing the land, Jeremiah offered a prayer of trust in God's sovereignty.

Moving to a new country, going to school, and starting a family was difficult. But as I look back over the last thirty years, I see evidence of God's faithfulness. He calmed our anxieties and provided for us beyond our wildest imagination. He helped us settle in a new culture and blessed us with children, friends, a church family, and jobs.

What new beginnings do you face? Perhaps you are in transition or facing a difficult situation and have many unanswered questions. Take heart, for the same God who guided Jeremiah and the Israelites will guide you. He loves you and sees your situation. He will not let you down. You can trust him to guide your steps.

Prayer

It is difficult to trust
when we face transition and uncertainties.
When life feels impossible,
help us trust you to know
that you will fulfill your promises.
Amen.

Put On the Full Armor

Put on the full armor of God,
so that you can take your stand
against the Devil's schemes.
EPHESIANS 6:11

I was waiting in my car for a friend. Suddenly a white car pulled up in the parking lot across from me. The driver was a woman. She got out of her car, and then a man and a teenage boy joined her. The three of them talked for a while before the man and boy walked off.

The woman opened her trunk and pulled out a vest. Later, I realized it was a bulletproof vest. Next, she wrapped a duty belt around her waist with weapons already in place. She tugged on her bulletproof vest again to check the fit and position. Then she got in her car and drove away.

As she drove off, the Scripture in Ephesians 6:11 came to mind. I had just observed a woman put on her full armor before going to work as a security guard.

How do we prepare for life's storms? When trouble comes knocking at our door, do we have the right tools and equipment?

Like the security guard's armor, God provides his children with spiritual armor so we can stand against the Enemy's schemes. His full armor comprises the belt of truth buckled around the waist, the breastplate of righteousness, feet fitted with the readiness that comes with the gospel of peace, the shield of faith, the helmet of salvation, and the sword of the spirit, which is the Word of God—

and prayer.

The security woman prepared by putting on her bulletproof vest and duty belt with her weapons. The passage in Ephesians 6 reminds us that our struggles are not against flesh and blood but against spiritual forces of evil. Not having the proper tools will lead to defeat.

God did not promise a life without stress. When we face challenges, we are tempted to react or use escape mechanisms to overcome our overwhelming feelings. Perhaps we resort to shopping, overeating, watching TV, or other types of activities to provide temporary relief.

Our battles are spiritual. If we put on God's armor, we can stand strong in the Lord and in his mighty power.

Prayer

Lord, thank you for the example
of the security guard.
Help me put on your full armor
in the form of prayer, worship,
and meditating on your Word daily
so I may overcome the Enemy's traps.
Amen.

Consistent Connection

Let me hear of your unfailing love each morning,
for I am trusting you.
Show me where to walk,
for I give myself to you.
PSALM 143:8 NLT

Early one morning, when my husband was leaving for work, I escorted him outside to see him off. When I turned around to go back inside, I caught a glimpse of the bright sky and the shining moon. I stopped for a moment and thanked God for another new day and for eyes to behold his lovely creation.

If we are open to it, we can learn many lessons from adversity. Some lessons I have learned include self-discipline, increased awareness, and appreciation of God's beautiful creation.

I did not always have a consistent prayer routine, but dealing with difficult situations helped me create new habits and embrace self-discipline. With time, the practice of getting up early in the morning to connect with God through singing hymns, reading his Word, and meditation became easier. When I neglect this time with God, I feel like something is missing.

I love to walk or jog outdoors regularly. Some days I pair my exercise with spending time with God. As I exercise, I listen to worship music, listen to Scripture, or pray. This practice creates variety and ensures that I am consistent in spending time with God in the morning.

God loves to connect with his children. It shows we love him and depend on him to order our steps.

How often do you connect with God? In what ways have you experienced his unfailing love? There is something special about maintaining a consistent connection with God. His steadfast love never ceases, and his mercies never end. They are new every morning. Great is his faithfulness (Lamentations 3:22–23.)

Cultivating a routine of connecting with the Lord will prepare you ahead of any storms that may come during the day and provide you strength to withstand.

Prayer

Lord, I desire to have
a consistent connection with you.
Help me to rise early
and embrace the discipline
of spending time with you.
Amen.

Pity Party

Rather, clothe yourselves
with the Lord Jesus Christ,
and do not think about
how to gratify the desires of the flesh.
ROMANS 13:14

How do we gratify the desires of the flesh? Sometimes when we face difficulties, we focus on our circumstances. It is easy to embrace a victim mentality and have a pity party because things are not going the way we expect.

Romans 13:14 reminds us to clothe ourselves with Jesus Christ and let go of the victim mentality. Rather than go into survival mode or numb our pain with all kinds of fleshly desires such as alcohol, drugs, or other mindless activities, we are to allow God's Word to guide our responses.

During a time when my marriage was in crisis, I was in so much emotional pain I gave in to self-pity. I felt alone and did not know how to navigate this marital crisis.

Although I had friends and mentors who encouraged me, it was while reading my Bible that I had an aha moment. As I read Romans 13:14 and reflected on its meaning, I realized that clothing myself with Christ meant changing my mindset to align with God's Word.

As I gained God's perspective, I decided to literally clothe myself with God's Word. I wrote Scriptures on three-by-five cards and placed them on my bathroom mirror. Every morning while dressing, I read the verse on each card aloud. I wanted my soul to soak in God's truth. Throughout the day, I meditated on these Scriptures.

This practice transformed my mindset, and I slowly went from feeling sorry for myself to feeling empowered by Christ.

Our help is not in the bottle or any other fleshly desires. Our help comes from God. As we clothe ourselves with him, we can be sure of divine guidance and relief.

Prayer

Lord, when life throws a curve ball at me,
remind me of your Word
and empower me to soak in its truth.
Thank you for loving me through your Word.
Amen.

He Will Not Let Your Foot Slip

He will not let your foot slip—
he who watches over you will not slumber.

PSALM 121:3

At some point in life, each of us will face temptations that cause us to compromise our values or take shortcuts. These temptations are more common when we are the most vulnerable.

My friend was facing a serious illness. One day another friend and I stopped by to check on him. While praying with him, I had all kinds of crazy thoughts. I could not wait to get out of there. I knew this was the Enemy trying to trip me.

Jesus also faced temptation. He was in the desert fasting and praying for forty days and forty nights (Matthew 4:1–11). The devil knew Jesus was fasting and tempted him by asking him to turn stones into bread to satisfy his hunger. But Jesus responded, "Man shall not live by bread alone, but by every word that comes from the mouth of God" (Matthew 4:4 ESV). With every response Jesus gave, the devil came back with more temptations. Each time, Jesus responded with God's truth and did not fall for the devil's tricks.

As soon as I left my friend's house, I prayed and asked God to give me wisdom for how to help my friend without compromising my values. The Lord whispered in my spirit to reach out to him in other ways.

How do you deal with temptations? The Enemy loves to trip us up. Perhaps you are dealing with a difficult situation, and he is tempting you to take shortcuts. Don't give in to those temptations. He is looking to sabotage you. If you give in, he will turn around and accuse you and make you feel worthless. It is not worth it.

Just like Jesus, trust that God is with you. Call on him. He will answer. His eyes watch over those who do right, and his ears are open to their cries for help (Psalm 34:15). God will not allow your foot to slip and fall into the Enemy's snares. His ears are always open to the groans and cries of your heart.

Prayer

Lord, I confess the times
when I was tempted to take offense, retaliate,
or act in ways contrary to your ways.
Forgive me, Lord,
and help me make wise decisions
that keep me on your path.
Amen.

Whatever Concerns You Concerns Him

So God looked on the Israelites
and was concerned about them.

EXODUS 2:25

We rarely get a lot of snow in our area in the winter, but one year we had three snowstorms in less than three weeks. One day when we were snowed in, my husband came home from work and mentioned that some trash bags were on the ground near my car. I asked my daughter if she knew anything about the bags.

She said, "Yes, I placed them there in the morning when I heard it would snow again. I did not want you to fall when you go to the car to drive to work." Besides laying the bags on the ground and securing them with stones, she'd cleared my windshield.

Our driveway is on a slope, and I have fallen many times during bad weather. On several occasions this winter, she watched me from the front door as I went down our treacherous driveway to my car at the bottom of the hill. My daughter's actions were out of her concern for my safety. Her love filled my heart with joy.

This event reminds me of God's care for me through others. It also reminds me of how God showed his concern for the Israelites in Egypt. The children of Israel migrated to Egypt because of famine in the land. Their brother Joseph was in charge of food supplies, so he encouraged them to move to Egypt. Over several generations, the

Israelites grew into a great nation, and with changes in government, they became slaves and faced all kinds of cruelty and hard labor for four hundred years.

Their conditions were so bad that the Israelites cried out to the Lord. The Lord heard their cries and was moved with compassion. God delivered the Israelites through Moses and fulfilled his promise to Abraham (Genesis 15:13–14).

In what ways have you experienced God's love and care?

Prayer

Lord, you are a gracious Father
who is concerned about all your children.
Thank you for the assurance
that I can always count on you to have my back.
In Jesus's name.
Amen.

Hand Over Your Deepest Longings

In her deep anguish,
Hanna prayed to the Lord,
weeping bitterly.
1 SAMUEL 1:10

During my late teens, I used to imagine what it would be like to marry and have children. Many times I daydreamed about getting married to a handsome man and imagined our life together would be filled with love. I longed to marry a good Christian man and have a family, so I prayed regularly for my future husband.

Hannah also longed to have children. Being the first wife, she was in a favorable situation, but her barrenness made it difficult to enjoy her position. She longed to have children just like her husband's second wife, Peninnah, who had several sons and daughters. Hannah's barrenness notwithstanding, her husband Elkanah doted on her. Every year when the family went to Shiloh to worship at the temple, he gave her a double portion of meat for the sacrifice.

Unfortunately, Peninnah would remind Hannah of her barrenness and provoke her to the point of crying. Hannah's tears became her food day and night (Psalm 42:3–4). Even her husband could not console her.

One day while everyone else was feasting and drinking at

Shiloh, Hannah took her case to the Lord. In deep anguish, she wept bitterly as she prayed and made a vow. She vowed that if the Lord would give her a son, she would dedicate him to the Lord's service.

Hannah shifted her focus, let go of bitterness and resentment, and gave her longings to God. She chose the Lord as her refuge and prayed boldly and specifically for a son. In due time, the Lord answered Hannah's prayer. She gave birth to a son and named him Samuel (which means *heard by God*). When Samuel was three years old, she brought him to the temple and dedicated him to the service of the Lord. Samuel grew up to become a great prophet and leader in Israel.

What is your deepest longing? Imagine what could happen if you handed your deepest longing over to God.

Prayer

Lord, I know that you love me,
and you desire to fulfill my longings
according to your purpose.
Help me submit my longings to you
and trust you with the outcome.
Amen.

Abiding:
There Is a Purpose in the Storm

I am the vine; you are the branches.
Whoever abides in Me, and I in him,
he it is that bears much fruit,
for apart from Me you can do nothing.
JOHN 15:5 ESV

I struggled to make sense of it all. I must have asked the Lord *why?* a million times. The more I asked this question, the more frustrated I became. Why would a loving God allow me to go through this crisis and heartache? I wrestled with him for a long time with no answers.

Perhaps like me, you are questioning the purpose of your storm and would prefer for it to be over fast. We struggle because we don't understand the meaning of our storm and what God is doing.

God has a purpose in our storms. Peter, one of the three disciples closest to Jesus, failed when he denied Jesus three times: when he spoke impulsively out of turn, when he lacked faith and nearly drowned, and when he couldn't keep awake to pray with Jesus. Peter was disappointed with himself and went back to fishing after Jesus's death. Why did God permit Peter to fail so many times?

Our storms are sometimes God's way of pruning us in preparation to bear more fruit. Storms help us depend on God and grow in faith. Peter's storms allowed God to prune him in preparation for a deeper faith. Subsequently, he led three thousand people to Christ in one day (Acts 2:41).

After years of wrestling with God, I finally understood the concept of abiding with him in the storm. I didn't resist the process anymore and allowed God to show me his purpose by abiding in him. I woke up early to read my Bible, pray, and reflect. I wrote any insights I received in my journal. By abiding, I gained a new perspective, which made the hardships and pruning bearable.

What is God doing in your storm, and where do you see him working? God's purpose is for us to bear more fruit. The process of pruning is painful but necessary for our growth. Abiding allows us to trust God in the process.

Prayer

Thank you for being the true vine
and that you call me to abide in you.
I want to bear fruit.
However, I know it won't happen without pruning.
Help me, Lord, to surrender my will
so you may do the work in me
to make me more fruitful for your kingdom.
Amen.

He Watches over You

The Lord will keep you from all harm—
he will watch over your life.

PSALM 121:7

I woke up to the sound of my roommate calling my name. There was a noise outside that sounded as if someone was trying to come in through the tin roof. Initially I was scared as I tried to imagine what would happen to us if whoever was on the roof broke through. Then I remembered the dream I had before we went on this mission trip.

I reached over, grabbed my Bible, and took out copies of the hymns I brought from home. I sang "O Victory in Jesus" and then prayed until I felt at peace in my spirit. After about thirty minutes of prayer, I told my roommate, "I gave it to the Lord already, and I trust he is in control." I laid my head on the pillow and promptly fell asleep. My roommate told me later that shortly after I fell asleep, the noise stopped. We never found out who or what was on the roof. We slept peacefully each night for the rest of the trip.

It is easy to give in to fear when we face challenging situations. God calls us to have faith and to trust that he constantly watches over us. The same God who watched over the Israelites in the olden days is still our protector, defender, and shield in times of trouble.

How has the Lord watched over you in your trials? The good news is we can trust God to watch over us in every circumstance. He does not sleep or slumber (Psalm 121:4), so it is useless to stay up at night and worry. Trusting him means letting go of anxiety and worries.

Though I am still a work in progress, my trials have taught me to lean on God even when I do not understand. I am encouraged to know that God answers when I give him my cares and worries.

Friend, let us cast all our cares upon God and put our confidence in him.

Prayer

Lord, thank you that you are my protector
who does not sleep or slumber.
I confess I am anxious about my trials.
Help me trust you with my cares
and know that because you are in control,
I can sleep well at night.
Amen.

Beyond Words

Both Mahlon and Kilion also died,
and Naomi was left without her two sons and her husband.
RUTH 1:5

Have you ever found yourself in situations that left you speechless?

I visited a friend who lost her son at birth. As I walked into the hospital room, the atmosphere was heavy with grief. My friend and her husband sat next to a little crib, tears streaming down their faces as they looked at their dead son. I sat with them in their grief.

Naomi and her family moved to Moab for a better life, but their good fortune was short lived as calamity struck the family. Naomi was overcome with grief by the loss of her husband and sons. When Naomi went back to Bethlehem, the women welcomed her. She told them to call her Mara because she felt the Lord had made her life bitter (Ruth 1:11).

Perhaps, like Naomi, you are dealing with grief or face multiple challenges that leave you feeling defeated and speechless. Maybe, like Naomi, your focus is on the circumstances, and you do not see any hope.

Know that God is with you in your moments of frustration and despair. He does not condemn you for grieving. In fact, he made provision for it in the psalms.

Whenever I am in the pit, overwhelmed, and beyond words, I turn to Psalms to find words to help me express my feelings. Psalm 88 was a close companion as these words became the cry of my heart: "Oh God, my soul is full of trouble. I am like a person without strength. You have put me in the lowest pit, in the darkest depths" (see verses 3–6). This psalm helped me bare my soul to God without pretense.

In due time, God gave me his perspective, just as he did with Naomi. She gained God's perspective as she trusted his plan and provision for her through Ruth, her daughter-in-law. Later, when Naomi and others reflected on God's care of Naomi and Ruth, they praised the Lord (Ruth 4:14).

Look up, friend. God longs to hear the cries of your heart. Trust him to walk with you in the darkest pit.

Prayer

Lord, I know you are with me
in the darkest of depths.
Thank you for helping me express my anguish,
for hearing my cry, and for comforting me.
Thank you for giving me your perspective.
May you fill my mouth with praise.
Amen.

The Day the World Changed

I have no peace, no quietness;
I have no rest, but only turmoil.

JOB 3:26

August 9, 2007, marks the worst financial crisis since the Great Depression. As financial institutions collapsed, many faced the possibility of losing their jobs. Businesses went under, people were laid off, some faced foreclosure, and some lost their retirement savings. Many had trouble sleeping because of deep anguish. As the crisis got worse, the mental health crisis and suicide rates soared.[5]

Job could relate to this crisis. He was a rich man who was deeply committed to the Lord. One day, without warning, his entire world collapsed as a massive tsunami landed at his doorstep. One servant after another brought bad news. He lost his oxen, donkeys, sheep, and livestock. To make matters worse, a mighty wind struck the house where all his ten children were feasting, and they all died.

Job's initial response blows my mind every time I read it. "Naked I came from my mother's womb, and naked I will depart. The Lord gave, and the Lord has taken away; may the name of the Lord be praised" (Job 1:21).

As if these trials were not enough, Job was afflicted with painful sores all over his body. Job told his friends, "I have no peace, no quietness, no rest, but only turmoil." At the height of his pain, Job cursed the day he was born.

Can you relate to Job's anguish? What tsunamis and calamities are you facing? Perhaps a job loss, financial crisis, a health crisis, betrayal, divorce, or loss of a loved one?

We go through trials for various reasons, and we don't always understand why. The good news is God works through our trials to draw us closer to him. Job's trials deepened his character, knowledge, and dependence on God. Although Job did not find immediate relief in his suffering, he got a deeper perspective of God through humility, tears, and brokenness. In the end, God gave him a double-fold restoration of all his possessions, and Job responded, "My ears had heard of you but now my eyes have seen you" (Job 42:5).

When we face trials that rock our world, we can trust God like Job. God can use our trials to transform us if we will trust him with our fears and doubts.

Prayer

Lord, sometimes I grow weary
under the burden of so many trials.
Help me trust you to work through them
to reveal yourself in new ways.
Amen.

Call to Remembrance

I will remember the deeds of the Lord;
yes, I will remember
your miracles of long ago.
PSALM 77:11

I lay in bed unable to sleep as my mind raced with many thoughts. A heavy darkness threatened to pull me into a dark pit. In my foggy mind, I considered different scenarios as I weighed my choices—either to embrace the darkness and give in to self-pity or choose to remember.

After the Israelites crossed the Red Sea, the people recalled the miracles of God. They sang and praised Yahweh: "I will sing to the Lord, for he has triumphed gloriously; the horse and his rider he has thrown into the sea" (Exodus 15:1 ESV). Later, God commanded the Israelites to remember his faithfulness and teach it to future generations (Deuteronomy 4:9).

That night as I laid in bed, weary and troubled, I remembered all the ways God had been with me over the years.

- *Lord*, you were with me when the thief broke into my dorm in high school and held a knife to my throat. You protected me.
- *Lord*, when I left home and moved to a new country, you were there. You guided me and helped me make new friends.
- *When my dad* passed away at a young age and left me to care for my mom and siblings, Lord, you were there. You gave me wisdom and provided for us.

- *Lord,* from a young age when I accepted Jesus as my Savior, you promised never to forsake me or leave me alone.
- *When I had* my first child, and had no experience, you brought people into my life to help me.

As I remembered God's faithfulness in the past, more memories of his tender care flooded my soul and chased away the darkness. I welcomed the light of God's embrace. This habit of remembrance has kept me out of the pit of hopelessness and helped me weather many storms.

How has God been faithful to you? God wants us to remember and recall his faithfulness. Try it. When next you are overwhelmed, anxious, or depressed, remember specific instances of God's grace, and speak your gratitude aloud to him.

Prayer

Lord, thank you for all the ways
you provided and cared for me in the past,
I trust you with my life
in the present and future.
Amen.

Peace Redefined

Peace I leave with you, my peace I give you.
I do not give to you as the world gives.
Do not let your hearts be troubled and do not be afraid.

JOHN 14:27

What is your definition of peace?

A few years ago, I adopted the practice of asking the Lord for a word at the beginning of the year. For 2015 my word was *peace*. As I thought about the word, I expected rest, tranquility, and an end to our long, drawn-out trials. As if to confirm my word, one of my students gave me a Christmas ornament with a peace symbol. I hung it in my office as a reminder of my word for the year.

Jesus promised his disciples peace, the kind that would stay with them in every situation. In John 16:33 Jesus said, "I have told you these things so that in me you may have peace. In this world you will have trouble. But take heart! I have overcome the world." Jesus's peace is different from the world's peace. It is a deep, abiding, and unwavering peace that is only found in him. Though we may experience troubles in this world, Jesus assures us of his peace.

One day I found my ornament shattered in pieces on the floor. Looking back, the broken ornament was a metaphor of what was to come. Our lives took on new twists and turns beyond our imaginations. My family experienced multiple car accidents, job loss, and serious health issues. Then to top it all, our house caught on fire due to lightning from a thunderstorm. We were homeless.

This was not peace as I expected.

Through this experience, I gained a deeper understanding of true peace. God's peace sustained us under the weights of multiple challenges. Despite the trials, we had joyful moments, such as graduation from college and a miraculous provision of a temporary home. In all, we experienced God's love in new ways as he redefined peace for us.

My definition of peace has changed radically. Peace no longer means calm, without conflict. It is a matter of standing still and trusting God wholeheartedly in the middle of very difficult circumstances. True peace is only available in him for all who will receive it.

Prayer

Lord, you are the Prince of Peace
who will sustain me
when I am hard pressed by life's trials.
Thank you for enabling me to endure and rest
in the assurance of your comfort.
Amen.

Banquet

You prepare a feast for me
in the presence of my enemies.
PSALM 23:5 NLT

As I reflect on this verse in Psalms, a picture of my family at dinner while on a cruise comes to mind. The table was elegant, set with fine china and silverware. Two waiters were on hand to provide world-class service. We took our seats, and after some small talk, the waiters served soup, which was the first of a five-course meal. To tell you the truth, my family was not excited about this meal. The sight of the food alone threatened to spill the contents of our stomach out on the table. We were seasick and could not eat anything. I don't remember what was on the menu, but I remember how pitiful we felt and looked.

In Psalm 23, God tells us he has prepared a feast for his children, and he invites all to the table regardless of our trials and circumstances. This royal feast includes an abundance of peace, joy, long-suffering, meekness, kindness, goodness, self-control, love, and salvation.

But just as my family could not eat the banquet on the cruise because of seasickness, our heart's attitude and response to adversity can prevent us from partaking of God's rich banquet. If we give in to resentment, bitterness, unforgiveness, strife, envy, jealousy, self-pity, selfishness, and other works of the flesh, we won't enjoy what God sets before us.

Earlier in my marriage, I could not fully enjoy God's royal feast because of my heart's attitude. I was easily offended, quick to blame others, and harbored resentment. A crisis in my marriage drew me closer to God. It was during this painful time that God showed me things in my heart that prevented me from feasting on his banquet and enjoying a full-course meal. One by one I surrendered attitudes such as bitterness and resentment. I asked God to help me love myself and others with his love. For me, this is an ongoing process of confession, repentance, forgiveness, and surrender. This is what helps me eat the royal meal at God's table.

What is holding you back from partaking of the Lord's banquet and feasting like a child of the King?

Prayer

Lord, sometimes my attitude prevents me
from dining at your table.
Cleanse my heart of all sinful attitudes.
Thank you for your love and the invitation
to dine like a princess at your table.
Amen.

Stand Firm and Be Still

May your God, whom you serve continually,
rescue you!
Daniel 6:16

Have you ever been the target of envy and jealousy?

Daniel performed his duties with excellence and stood out among his peers. He prayed at least three times a day. Because of his integrity and relationship with God, his colleagues plotted evil against him out of envy and jealousy.

They asked King Darius to make a decree that no one could pray to any man or god for thirty days except to the king. Though Daniel knew of this law, he kept his usual prayer pattern. Because of this, they threw him in the lions' den.

Perhaps you can identify with Daniel. Sometimes we find ourselves in difficult circumstances through no fault of our own. For instance, Daniel's prayer life got him in trouble. For me, gaining God's perspective in my trials and developing a deeper relationship with him made some people feel threatened. They saw the changes in me but couldn't stand it, so they ridiculed me.

What do you do when you find yourself in a similar situation? The Enemy would love nothing more than for us to compromise our values. He will tempt us to complain, grumble, retaliate, or cave in to the pressure to please others. Don't do it. Just be still.

Daniel was still in the lions' den, and God protected him. God sent an angel to shut the mouths of the lions. When he came out from the lions' den, Daniel was not hurt and had no wounds, all because he trusted God.

Faced with afflictions and false accusations, we must stand firm and trust God. The Lord himself will fight for us; we only need to be still (Exodus 14:14). Just as God delivered Daniel, he will deliver you, and your testimony will bring others to Christ.

Because of Daniel's faithfulness to God, the pagan king Darius believed in the God of heaven and made a new decree that all the people must fear and worship the God of Daniel.

How will your response to false accusations draw others to Christ?

Prayer

You are the living God
who is mighty to save.
Help me not to give in
to the attacks of the Enemy.
Give me an unshakable faith
that draws others to you.
Amen.

Living Gracefully with Difficult People

Ishmael will be like a wild donkey.
He will be against everyone,
and everyone will be against him.
He will attack all his brothers.
GENESIS 16:12 NCV

Recently I came across a porcupine sculpture my son made in elementary school. Seeing this sculpture reminded me of the difficult people in my life. Getting close to them can sometimes mean getting hurt. Just like spikes on the porcupine, their words can be sharp.

Do you have difficult people in your life? How often do you wish they would change? Often, my prayer is, *Change them, Lord.* I want them to stop being so impossible. Why do they irritate me so?

Then I found this definition of a difficult person in Genesis 16:12: "He will be against everyone, and everyone will be against him. He will attack all his brothers." Can you imagine what it would be like living with this personality?

As I reflected on this verse, I realized difficult people are prewired with a bent toward seeing the glass as half-empty. This predisposition to be difficult and hostile can make them get under our skin.

These insights challenged me to rethink my view of the difficult people in my life. I asked the Lord to speak to my heart and help me see them through his eyes. He showed me they have a purpose.

Like the porcupine's spiky exterior, difficult people appear mean on the surface, but their hostility is a cover for their soft, vulnerable interior. Living with difficult people requires having healthy boundaries and giving them plenty of grace. They need understanding, love, and acceptance—especially if we want to point them to Jesus.

Difficult people challenge me to see my own gaps. God uses them like sandpaper to smooth out my rough edges. Recognizing that I could be someone else's difficult person has changed my heart's cry to *Change me, Lord. Change me.* My desire is to model 1 John 4:12 to the difficult people in my life: "If we love each other, God lives in us and his love is made perfect in us" (NCV).

Will you ask Jesus to love the difficult people in your life through you?

Prayer

Lord, sometimes it is challenging
to love the difficult people in my life.
Help me embrace the challenges they bring
as opportunities to grow.
Show me how to love them
and help me love them with your love.
Amen.

Adapting to Change

*"I am the Lord's servant," Mary answered.
"May your word to me be fulfilled."*
LUKE 1:38

Patience is hard for me. I like to have a plan, but I feel frustrated when those plans change or get interrupted. As I am getting older, the Lord is teaching me patience, flexibility, and how to trust him more.

Mary was a virgin, engaged to be married to Joseph, when she found herself pregnant through the Holy Spirit. The angel of the Lord appeared to her and told her she would give birth to a son named Jesus. She pondered these things in her heart. She was open to God's plan and direction (Luke 1:26–38).

According to the custom of that day, Joseph had plans to put Mary away after he found out she was pregnant. But the angel of the Lord visited Joseph and told him to take Mary as his wife, for she was carrying the Lord (Matthew 1:18–25). Mary and Joseph are a courageous couple who model for us what it looks like to adapt to change and trust God to reshape plans according to his purpose.

In what ways can you be more open to change?

Often, trials compel us to evaluate our situation and make adjustments. Perhaps, like me, you find change difficult and need reassurance. Mary asked questions of the angel, but she chose to trust God's plan.

Through the crisis in my marriage, I learned to trust God even when I did not know how things would work out. My willingness to be adaptable allowed God to work in my heart and reveal his greater purpose for my husband and me. No matter the challenges we face, giving control over to the Lord and trusting Him with the outcome is the best choice.

Our willingness to change in times of adversity provides opportunities to gain God's perspective and see him at work.

Prayer

Father, help me to trust and obey you.
Allow your Holy Spirit to guide my steps.
Thank you for reshaping my plans
according to your will and purpose.
Thank you for your power to flow in your Spirit.
Amen.

Guard Your Heart

Above all else, guard your heart,
for everything you do flows from it.

PROVERBS 4:23

Have you ever blurted out words you later regretted? Our words often reflect what we are thinking.

Just as water reflects the face, so our words reflect our heart. Guarding our hearts means to guard our spiritual hearts. Your heart and mind are the inner core responsible for your thoughts, feelings, desires, will, and choices.

The children of Israel experienced God's mighty deliverance from slavery in Egypt. But as they traveled through the wilderness in the desert, they soon forgot what God had done for them. They complained and grumbled because, despite their misery in Egypt, they missed the security of their former life.

Like the Israelites, it is easy to let our thoughts stray as we focus on our circumstances during times of adversity. Perhaps someone has offended us or treated us unfairly, so we feel justified to think ill of them or, worse yet, gossip about them. Often our wrong attitudes and actions toward others stem from having impure thoughts.

We may believe no one knows what we are thinking, but God does. When we allow fear and anxiety to creep in and overwhelm us, we forget our experiences of God's goodness and faithfulness. Though our present circumstances may be difficult, God is working through them to make all things work together for our good. We must ask God to help us have pure thoughts.

How can we guard our hearts?

Guarding our hearts means seeing our situation from God's viewpoint and being in frequent communication with him through prayer. It means living in submission and obedience to God's will. Guarding our hearts requires us to intentionally focus our hearts away from foolish talk, murmuring, grumbling, and complaining, and toward pure, noble, God-honoring thoughts (Philippians 2:13–14).

Another way to guard our hearts is through meditating on the following Scriptures:

> Create in me a pure heart, O God, and renew a steadfast spirit within me. Do not cast me from your presence or take your Holy Spirit from me. Restore to me the joy of your salvation, and grant me a willing spirit, to sustain me. (Psalm 51:10–12)

> Search me, God, and know my heart; test me and know my anxious thoughts. See if there is any offensive way in me, and lead me in the way everlasting. (Psalm 139:23–24)

When we meditate on these Scriptures, we can invite God to reveal any impure thoughts and cleanse our hearts.

Prayer

Father, help me to change my thoughts
and keep my mind focused
on where you are working in my life.
Give me a mind that thinks pure thoughts
and reflects Christ.
Amen.

Sufficient Grace

"My grace is sufficient for you,
for my power is made perfect in weakness."
Therefore, I will boast all the more gladly about my weaknesses,
so that Christ's power may rest on me.
2 Corinthians 12:9

As a young seventeen-year-old girl, Joni Eareckson Tada's future looked bright and promising. Nevertheless, a diving accident in 1967 left her paralyzed from the neck down, changing the course of her life. She went through months of therapy and bouts of depression. She prayed for healing, but God did not answer as she anticipated.

Sometimes God does not answer the way we ask because he has something better in mind. Lazarus was sick. His sisters, Mary and Martha, sent word to Jesus that Lazarus was sick. But Jesus delayed, and Lazarus died. The sisters were grief stricken and could not understand why Jesus waited. They did not understand that Jesus had a better plan. It was not to save Lazarus in his current condition but to raise him from the dead. Many who witnessed that story believed in Jesus.

While God did not remove Joni's quadriplegia, he answered her prayers. He called her to serve others with disabilities and bring glory to God through her weakness. Her ministry, Joni and Friends, is vibrant and ministers to people with disabilities all over the world. Through her ministry, she distributes wheelchairs to the disabled and shares the love of Jesus with them. Joni has visited over one hundred countries, donated more than fifty thousand wheelchairs, and written over fifty books. Several of her books have been translated into thirty-five or more languages. She also hosts a radio program and a television series.

Although our trials seem big to us, God can use them to bring good beyond our imagination. He can answer in ways that bring out the best in us. Just as the greater blessing and miracle was in raising Lazarus from the dead, the blessing of Joni's quadriplegia allows her to share the gospel and turn many hearts to believe in Jesus. We, too, can trust God with our trials.

What are you waiting on God for? How will you trust God's plan for your life in this season?

Prayer

Lord, I confess that waiting is hard,
and trusting you to work things out is even harder.
Help me to trust your plan when life gets tough.
Please grant me the grace to wait on you
as you work to bring out the best in my situation.
Amen.

Patient Endurance

Consider it pure joy, my brothers and sisters,
whenever you face trials of many kinds,
because you know that the testing of your faith
produces perseverance.
JAMES 1:2–3

How is it possible to endure gruesome trials and be joyful?

At one time, I did not fully understand the meaning of this verse in James. However, facing homelessness and other trials of immense proportions taught me about the importance of having the right attitude and growing through trials.

Paul faced many hardships in his ministry. He was imprisoned, shipwrecked, beaten, and endured a persistent thorn in the flesh. Though we do not know the nature of his thorn in the flesh, he pleaded with God to remove it. Rather than remove the thorn, God's response was, "My grace is sufficient for you, for my power is made perfect in weakness" (2 Corinthians 12:9). This suggests God had other plans for Paul and his thorn.

We know Paul served the Lord fervently. Perhaps without the thorn, Paul would not have served the Lord as he should. Throughout his ministry, Paul looked consistently to the Lord to help him withstand the adversities and persecutions he faced. The multiple trials helped Paul persevere.

There is a saying that the only way out is through. When we face trials, we can adopt a victim mentality or we can lean on God to carry us through. He promises to be with us when we walk through the valley of the shadow of death. Our trials can make us stronger as we allow God to use our struggles to build our faith. He wants us to be persistent in prayer and keep our eyes focused on Him (James 1:2–3).

What trials are you facing today? How will you allow God to strengthen your faith as you patiently persevere?

Prayer

Father, when I am faced with life's challenges,
I need you to remind me to count it all joy.
Help me persevere
as you work through the trials
to increase my faith.
Amen.

Walking in Wisdom and Humility

If you are wise and understand God's ways,
prove it by living an honorable life,
doing good works with the humility
that comes from wisdom.

JAMES 3:13 NLT

Abigail was a beautiful and wise woman who loved God and her family. She found joy in serving her family and working alongside the servants who helped her husband with the livestock. But life at home could be challenging because her husband was difficult and erratic.

Nabal was rich. He owned several properties and a large flock of sheep and goats, but everyone in the town considered him a rude, mean, and arrogant man. One time during the sheep-shearing season, David sent his men to ask for food in exchange for protecting his livestock, but Nabal mocked, insulted, and ridiculed them (1 Samuel 25:2–11).

When Abigail heard of her husband's behavior toward David and his men, she took immediate action to rectify the situation. She loaded a donkey with food and sent a servant to deliver it ahead of her. As she got on her donkey to go and meet David, I imagine Abigail recalling the previous times she had to manage the tension created by her husband's behavior. Perhaps she said a quick prayer asking for wisdom.

She used wisdom in talking David off the ledge, and her wisdom, humility, and quick intervention prevented David from taking revenge on her family. She confronted her husband with humility when she told him how his actions put his family in danger (1 Samuel 25:14–38). Abigail made the best of a difficult marriage and relied on God's wisdom and humility to guide her.

Perhaps you are in a difficult marriage or relationship. What challenges are you facing? How will you make the best of your situation?

God desires to guide and help us navigate any problems we face in our marriages and relationships. Like Abigail, you and I can trust God for wisdom and discernment to handle the challenging relationships with love, humility, and grace.

Prayer

Lord, grant me the desire
to walk in wisdom and humility in my relationship
with my spouse, family, and others.
Help me see others through the eyes of your love
and trust in your power to change my difficult situations.
Amen.

My Only Hope Is in You

And so, Lord, where do I put my hope?
My only hope is in you.
PSALM 39:7 NLT

My team and I were pursuing a new line of work. I felt good about the project, and it seemed everyone on my team was on board with the plans. A few months into our venture, a key member of my team was hired by one of my collaborators. The lead person quit about the same time. The work was in jeopardy because the knowledge of these two team members was crucial for its success.

As I evaluated the situation, I felt blindsided and frustrated. It would take months to hire and train new staff. I had many unanswered questions. Have you ever asked a question and then tried to come up with your own answers?

Many times, when I find myself in the middle of a chaotic situation and I am at the end of my resources, I ask myself questions such as, "What are you going to do? Will you give in to self-pity and despair or trust God? How do I go forward with this project?"

When David faced a tough situation, rather than embrace despair, he affirmed his hope in God. He reflected on God's faithful character and trusted him with his present circumstances.

For my work situation, I followed David's example to seek God's guidance and put my hope in him. I recalled how God helped me in the past when I had to make major decisions concerning my work.

Sometimes when our plans are disrupted and we don't see a way out, remembering God's faithfulness in the past helps us trust that if God did it before, he will do it again. God's hope is an anchor that is strong and trustworthy when we face sudden changes.

What is your response to unexpected changes in your plans? How will you place your hope in God?

Prayer

Father, you know how sudden changes
can throw me for a loop.
Thank you that I can trust your character
during these times.
Thank you for putting your hope
in my spirit and your praise on my lips.
Amen.

Unload Your Burdens

Give your burdens to the Lord, and he will take care of you.
He will not permit the godly to slip and fall.
PSALM 55:22 NLT

One day during my morning walk, I saw a tree bent over with a heavy accumulation of snow and several broken branches. Seeing that tree reminded me of a friend who felt weighed down by worry and fear. My friend was dealing with a cancer diagnosis, no health insurance, and caring for two young children. Her situation was dire.

None of us are immune to life's problems. Our burdens can range from financial crisis, depression, alcoholism, addictions, family dysfunction, job loss, or a health crisis to issues with teenage children. When we feel overloaded with burdens, we may be tempted to embrace worry, anxiety, and fear. Worry adds nothing to our lives, and it robs us of inner peace.

Jesus understands, and he wants to help. He calls us to unload our burdens on him and reminds us to forsake our worries. "So don't worry about these things, saying, 'What will we eat? What will we drink? What will we wear?' These things dominate the thoughts of unbelievers, but your heavenly Father already knows all your needs" (Matthew 6:31–32 NLT).

As I thought of ways to encourage my friend, I prayed with her and shared these Scriptures. While her situation did not change overnight, she learned to go to God in prayer and trust him for her needs. My friend saw God's miraculous provision on many fronts. God provided doctors who advocated for her to get subsidies to cover the expensive medications for her cancer treatment. God provided a special friend who had experienced cancer to come alongside her. She received an outpouring of love and financial support from her community of faith. Friends volunteered to help with her children.

When my friend unloaded her burdens on Jesus, she found relief and realized that Jesus is more than sufficient. No matter the size of our burdens, God's promise is that he will sustain us and never leave us. It is only in Jesus we find relief from our burdens.

What heavy burdens are you willing to unload and trust Jesus with today?

Prayer

Father, forgive me for yielding
to the temptations of worry and fear.
Remind me to unload my cares on you
when I feel stressed.
Thank you for sustaining me
with your strength and power.
Amen.

Winning Over an Unbelieving Spouse

In the same way,
you wives must accept the authority of your husbands.
Then, even if some refuse to obey the Good News,
your godly lives will speak to them without any words.
They will be won over by observing
your pure and reverent lives.

1 PETER 3:1–2 NLT

Are you married to an unbelieving spouse?

In her book *Surviving a Spiritual Mismatch in Marriage,* Leslie Strobel describes what life was like when her husband was an atheist. Frustrations, feelings of inadequacy, emotional isolation, loneliness, opposition, and conflict over a variety of issues from finances to child-rearing style created severe tension in their relationship.[7]

Being married to an unbelieving spouse can be frustrating and disappointing, even if the spouse is excellent in many other areas. Perhaps like Leslie, you desire to share your faith with your unbelieving husband. Maybe you feel you are responsible for his unbelief.

Peter reminds us that we can still love our spouses even when they don't share our faith. We can win them over by our attitudes and through serving and pursuing them with God's love. We won't win them over by outward beauty, fine clothes, or jewelry alone but by our gentle spirit, or "holy beauty."

With the support and encouragement of a godly mentor, Leslie eventually recognized that she was not responsible for her husband's faith. She loved him and prayed for him regularly while trusting the Holy Spirit to convict him in due time. Today, Leslie and her husband, Lee, are serving the Lord together.

Never doubt your decision to follow Jesus. As you live out your faith with sincerity and humility, remember to serve your husband as unto the Lord. Trust God to use your gentle witness to work on your husband's heart. There is always hope.

Ask your husband to share his needs in one or two areas. In what ways can you serve him in these areas?

Prayer

Heavenly Father, I confess my frustrations, fears,
and hurts over my mismatched marriage.
Please replace them
with your peace, contentment, and love.
Help me to love my husband with your love
while trusting you to work in his heart
and reveal yourself to him in due time.
Amen.

My Helper

So we can confidently say,
"The Lord is my helper; I will not fear;
what can man do to me?"

HEBREWS 13:6 ESV

One morning while I was out running, I saw a father and his two sons riding their bikes up a hill. The father and the older boy were way ahead, while the younger boy was farther behind. Suddenly the older brother rode back downhill, turned around, and waited for his younger brother to ride uphill.

Lazarus was sick. His sisters, Mary and Martha, sent someone to inform Jesus that his friend needed help. But Lazarus died. It was not until four days later that Jesus arrived at the scene. His sisters were in deep distress at the loss of their brother. While the situation looked hopeless, the sisters held a glimmer of hope as Martha said to Jesus, "Lord, if you had been here, my brother would not have died. But even now I know that whatever you ask from God, God will give you" (John 11:21–22 ESV).

Just like the older boy turned around to help his brother and encourage him as he rode his bike up the hill, Jesus comes alongside us as we ride up the difficult hills of life. No matter what storms or trials we face, he offers us encouragement and hope.

Jesus wept with Mary and Martha and then raised their brother from the dead. His delay was so that God's name would be glorified in their situation.

I don't know what hill you may climb today, but I want to

encourage you that our older brother Jesus is right there to help you navigate the rough terrains of life. He may delay, but don't let that discourage you. His timing is always perfect. The One who raised Lazarus from the dead can help us overcome fear, speak hope to the dead areas of our lives, and make us come alive in him. He is our helper.

Jesus will give us strength for every trial if we will believe and trust him. Do you believe this?

Prayer

Lord, help me sense your presence
as I climb the hilly terrains of life.
Thank you for being my protector and shield.
Amen.

Facing Persecution for Your Faith

Meanwhile, Saul was uttering threats with every breath and was eager to kill the Lord's followers.

ACTS 9:1 NLT

Many Christians are facing persecution for their faith in various parts of the world. In 2015 the abduction of young girls from a Christian school in Nigeria led to a major outcry.

Are you being persecuted because of your faith and beliefs? Saul was a zealous Pharisee who believed the old Mosaic law was the only religious belief, and he and others joined in to persecute followers of Jesus with a passion. He had permission from the Jewish leaders to arrest believers and prosecute them.

Maybe like these early believers, you face persecution because of your faith in Christ. Perhaps you are ridiculed and oppressed by those who do not share your beliefs or faith. This is even more painful if the persecution is coming from loved ones who mock and call you names, trying to tear you down.

As painful as this is, there is hope. God is a mighty deliverer and a God of justice. As Saul was on his way to persecute Christians one more time, God stopped him. There is a saying in my native language: Every day is for the thief; one day is for the owner. Saul's days of persecuting believers were up. Jesus arrested him on the way to Damascus:

He fell to the ground and heard a voice say to him, "Saul, Saul, why do you persecute me?"

"Who are you, Lord?"

"I am Jesus whom you are persecuting," he replied. "Now get up and go into the city, and you will be told what you must do." (Acts 9:4–6)

That day Saul's life was transformed. We, too, can entrust our persecutors into Jesus's hands. If he could arrest Saul, the chief persecutor of Christians, and turn him around, he can do the same for us.

As I have trusted God, I have seen him transform my persecutors and naysayers. I have seen him turn their lives around to serve Jesus. Many now ask me to pray for them.

Prayer

Lord, you call us to bless those who persecute us
and to love our enemies.
I praise you because all power belongs to you.
Thank you for your transforming power
that transcends all barriers, brings repentance,
and gently woos us to your love.
Amen.

Stretched beyond Capacity

They were at their wits' end.
Then they cried out to the Lord in their trouble,
and he brought them out of their distress.

PSALM 107:27–28

Have you ever been at your wits' end?

Perhaps you are stretched beyond capacity because of a marriage on the rocks, a bad report from the doctor, a teenager struggling with depression, or mounting debt and creditors calling. At times life can stretch us beyond our emotional and mental limits.

Jonah was fleeing from the Lord's assignment. He boarded a ship sailing for Tarshish, and soon there was a great wind on the sea. A violent storm threatened to break up the ship. The sailors were at their wits' end. They threw the cargo into the sea and called on the passengers to cry out to God. They found Jonah fast asleep below the deck and woke him. "How can you sleep? Get up and call on your God! Maybe he will take notice of us so that we will not perish" (Jonah 1:6).

Desperation can make us take drastic measures. These sailors feared for their lives and those of the passengers. They called on everyone to pray. When we are stretched to our limits and the situation is beyond our control, we can tap into the resources of our heavenly Father.

When we cry to the Lord in our distress, he promises to deliver us out of our troubles. We can trust the same God who delivered the Israelites out of slavery in Egypt and caused their oppressors to favor them and give them gifts of silver, gold, and clothing. He is on our side. God sees our troubles. He knows our heartaches. He wants to still our storms and deliver us from spiritual oppression by the Enemy.

The passengers and Jonah cried to the Lord, and he heard their prayers. Even before we call on him, God will hear and answer our prayers (Isaiah 65:24). When we are stretched to the limit, we can trust God.

Prayer

Father, thank you for your promises and assurance
when I face distresses in life.
Thank you that you are just a prayer away.
Help me stay connected to you always.
Amen.

Losing a Loved One

Good people pass away;
the godly often die before their time.
But no one seems to care or wonder why.
No one seems to understand
that God is protecting them from the evil to come.
ISAIAH 57:1 NLT

My father died unexpectedly at age fifty-seven. I was devastated because Dad was my hero. As a child, I secretly planned how I would take care of him when I grew up. In my mind, I planned trips and events with my dad. But then death snatched him away . . . just like that. For a while, it was hard to know what to feel or how to respond. Sometimes I felt numb. At other times my soul ached. Anger seemed like a reasonable emotion. I was mad at God for taking my dad at such a young age.

I reminded God of all the plans I'd made for Dad and me. *If you truly love me, why did you take my father?* This wrestling and soul unrest over my dad's death went on for years, until the day I stumbled upon this Scripture in Isaiah: "Good people pass away." Sometimes they are taken before their time. We rarely know why, but God knows because he is "protecting them from the evil to come."

As the words of the verse percolated in my soul, I recognized that God is sovereign. While I may not understand why my father died young and the evil the Lord prevented him from experiencing, I can trust that the Lord's plans are always good.

He allows me to use my experience to comfort others who have lost loved ones. One of my students recently lost her dad. He was the same age as my father. I could feel her pain and loss as I empathized with her and encouraged her.

Losing my father also helped prepare me for my mom's death. Last year I lost a dear friend, prayer partner, and sister in Christ. Losing a loved one is never easy. Though we miss them, we can trust God to help us in our grief.

How will you ask God to comfort you and use your grief to bless others?

Prayer

Lord, I am grateful
for the lives of my dad, mom, and friend
who have gone home to be with you.
Although I miss their gentle smiles, hugs,
and encouraging words,
they will always remain in my heart.
Thank you for the hope
of meeting them again in heaven
in your sweet presence.
Amen.

Expand Your Comfort Zone

But when I am afraid, I will put my trust in you.
PSALM 56:3 NLT

During the summer, my colleagues and I run a program for students. As part of the preparation, we plan team-building activities that include games, challenges, and trust-building activities to promote cooperation, communication, and recognition of the group's strengths and weaknesses.

Zip lining was the activity we chose one year. I am afraid of heights, so I did not look forward to taking part in this activity. It was obvious that several of the students had the same fear. I faced a dilemma. How could I motivate the students to take a risk I wasn't willing to take myself? The duplicity of the situation made me feel sick to my stomach.

Lord, I pleaded silently. *Please help the students to gain confidence and encourage them to take part in zip lining.*

I heard a gentle nudge in my spirit. *How about you? Do you trust me?*

I responded, *Lord, I trust you, but I am fearful of heights.*

My students were unaware of the background deal I was making with the Lord. Zip lining was a major challenge, because it required trust. It meant letting go of fear and trusting the professionals. Trusting that the zip lining gear would sustain our weight and we would not fall. It meant trusting God beyond what I could see.

I whispered yes as I stepped forward and chose to expand my comfort zone.

Similarly, our Christian walk calls us to step out of our comfort zones to enjoy true fellowship with God. It calls for complete trust and letting go of our fears. Our walk with Jesus requires us to trust he can sustain us as we zip through the challenges of life.

This is not an intellectual trust but a heart trust. It is a trust that lets go of all preconceived notions and depends on God. The kind that accepts our limitations and embraces the challenges life brings our way, knowing we have the absolute support of our heavenly Father.

This kind of trust takes our fellowship with God to a whole new level. Do you yearn for this trust?

Prayer

Lord, you know my strengths and weaknesses.
Help me overcome my fears
and trust you when I feel challenged.
Amen.

Wait with Patience

As for me since I am poor and needy,
let the Lord keep me in his thoughts.
You are my helper and my savior.
O my God do not delay.
PSALM 40:17 NLT

For some years, I hosted a women's Bible study in my home. One time a lady brought her friend who was married for years but could not get pregnant. She was tired of waiting. I can identify with my friend's anguish about waiting. During a time when troubles threatened to overwhelm me and I was tired, I cried out to God in prayer, *O Lord, you are my Savior and helper. Please do not delay.*

When we are bombarded by endless trials, we want them to be over. But time seems to move at a slow pace. God's view of time differs from our own. To God, a thousand years is just like a day or a watch in the night (Psalm 90:4). His timing is always perfect— never early and never late. God is a promise keeper, and all his promises come to pass. When Lazarus was dead for four days and it looked like all hope was gone, Jesus raised him from the dead. We might think Jesus was late but to God, his timing was perfect.

If your prayers don't seem to be answered yet, don't give up. Delay is not denial. Hold fast to God, and don't chase after other gods. Give God your frustrations and your need to know the details of how he will work things out. In time he will answer your prayers. He will amaze you as he stills your storm and gives you a new song of praise.

A few months after we prayed for my friend who couldn't get pregnant, I had a dream that she gave birth to a baby boy. I thanked the Lord for the revelation and the baby to come. It was not until two years later that she gave birth to a son. God is faithful to his promises.

How is God growing and stretching you in your season of waiting? Instead of fretting, thank him for all the ways he is working behind the scenes. Put your confidence and hope in God.

Prayer

Lord, when trouble surrounds me
and I can't see my way out,
help me put my confidence
in your unfailing love and faithfulness.
Fill me with your joy and peace
as you remind me of the wonders
you have performed in the past.
Lord, you are my refuge and strength.
Do not delay.
Amen.

I See You

How do you know about me?
JOHN 1:48 NLT

I was standing in line at the store waiting to pay for items. The woman ahead of me had her son and daughter with her. The girl was about three years old. She looked at me and smiled. I smiled back. Then she poked her head out from her mother's side and quickly pulled it back. So, for the next five minutes we played peekaboo. She hid her face by her mom's leg and then suddenly popped her face back into view. I responded by saying, "Peekaboo. I see you." As the little girl laughed, she made all of us in the line laugh too.

From a distance, Jesus saw Nathaniel standing under a fig tree. Philip invited Nathaniel to come and meet Jesus. As they approached, Jesus said, "Now here is a genuine son of Israel—a man of complete integrity." Nathaniel asked Jesus, "How do you know about me?" (John 1:47–48 NLT).

Do you believe Jesus sees you? In the same way he saw Nathaniel under the fig tree, he sees you. He sees your heartache, loneliness, and struggles. Even if others do not see you, Jesus sees you right where you are. His eyes are upon your ways, and he sees all your steps (Job 34:21).

God saw you before you were born, and he is aware of every detail of your life down to the number of hairs on your head. His thoughts toward you are good and precious. Because Jesus sees us, we can take comfort in his presence and delight in knowing he will never leave or forsake us even in the midst of a raging storm. As we follow him wholeheartedly, we will see him perform great things. He alone can fill our hearts with joy and our mouths with laughter during trials.

Prayer

Jesus, you are the Son of God.
Thank you that you know and see me.
Help me let go of fear and lean on you,
the Lord who sees me.
You are my Rock and Shield.
Amen.

Trust-Button Reset

*Would I ever bring this nation to the point of birth
and then not deliver it? asks the Lord.*

ISAIAH 66:9 NLT

A friend once told me, "I am wound tight." By this statement, he meant he liked to be in control and know what will happen and when it will happen. He likes predictability. There is nothing wrong with having structure and being predictable, but if carried to excess, we will miss out on God's blessings, because sometimes he orchestrates detours in our plans.

Controlling everything around us will not do us any good except to leave us anxious, weary, and worn out. If we are too wedded to our own ideas, we are being wise in our own eyes and not trusting God. Rather than relying on our own wisdom, Solomon encourages us to "trust in the Lord with all your heart and do not lean on your own understanding. In all your ways acknowledge him, and he will make straight your paths" (Proverbs 3:5–6 ESV).

Solomon is asking you and me to hit the reset button. To quit being wound tight. To trust God. I have loved ones who have professed Christ and are not walking with him. My heart aches for them to come back to the Lord. Sometimes I try so hard to *fix* them, but my efforts often backfire. As I grow in my faith, I realize that my part is to love these family members with the love of Jesus, speak the truth in love, and allow him to take care of their hearts. The salvation of my loved ones is God's business. My part is to love them and live out my faith.

I don't know your situation. Maybe you have a child or family member who is backsliding, a health crisis, a financial situation, or a troubled marriage. Whatever it might be, let's give up the need to control situations and fix others. Trust the Lord with all your concerns. Praise and thank him in advance for all the ways he is working behind the scenes. Let go, and watch him do the things you thought were impossible.

God can deliver us from all our troubles and give us wisdom, but relying on our own understanding will hinder our faith.

What do you need to relinquish control of today? Ask the Lord for help to let go of worry and to increase your trust.

Prayer

You are a mighty deliverer.
Nothing is too hard for you.
Deliver me from my need
to control others and situations around me.
Reset my trust button and strengthen my faith, Lord.
Help me to show your love
through my words and actions.
Amen.

God's Strategic Plan

*Do not give a war cry,
do not raise your voices,
do not say a word until the day I tell you to shout.
Then shout!*
JOSHUA 6:10

Do you enjoy planning? I like to have a plan and an idea of what to expect. I generally have a plan A and then plans B and C as backup. Most of the time, my plans don't work out as I expect.

To take possession of the land, the children of Israel had to conquer Jericho. They faced a challenge of how to tear down the fortified walls of the city. The Lord gave Joshua a simple strategic plan for capturing Jericho along with its king and fighting men.

> March around the city once with all the armed men. Do this for six days. Have seven priests carry trumpets of rams' horns in front of the ark. On the seventh day, march around the city seven times, with the priests blowing the trumpets. When you hear them sound a long blast on the trumpets, have the whole army give a loud shout; then the wall of the city will collapse and the army will go up, everyone straight in. (Joshua 6:3–5)

In case you are wondering what kind of plan this is, I am with you on that one. The plan makes no sense at all to my logical mind, but Joshua and the people obeyed. They marched around Jericho every day. On the seventh day at the sound of the trumpet and shouting, the walls of the city collapsed.

God's ways are not our ways, and his thoughts are not our thoughts. They are beyond anything we could imagine (Isaiah 55:8). Often God's plans may not make sense to us. But if we trust him with our trials and struggles, he will show us his strategic plan. With him on our side, we will overcome every storm.

Do you want God's strategic plan for your current trial? Let me encourage you to read your Bible, pray, and seek God. Stay in fellowship with other believers and live out your faith. When I faced a crisis in my marriage, I spent time with God in prayer and fasting. I also asked a friend to pray along with me. God is with us in our trials. He has a perfect plan for you and me.

Prayer

You hold the blueprint to my life.
Though I may be surrounded by difficult situations,
help me trust that your plans for me
are for good and not evil.
Bless you, Lord.
Amen.

Battle Weary

Never! Can a mother forget her nursing child?
Can she feel no love for the child she has borne?
But even if that were possible,
I would not forget you!

ISAIAH 49:15 NLT

How long will this storm last? If you are like me, life's storms that appear to go on with no end in sight can leave us battle weary. As I reflect on the many storms I have faced since 2007, I remember how fear threatened to overwhelm me. Many times, all I could see was the devastation and ruins as I thought I would never be happy again. I often wondered what God was up to and if he was paying attention to my crisis.

But the verse in Isaiah reminds us that God is like a mother who never forgets her children. "Like an eagle that rouses her chicks and hovers over her young, so he spread his wings to take them up and carried them safely on his pinions" (Deuteronomy 32:11 NLT).

During a time when my daughter faced a health crisis, the picture of God as an eagle spreading its wings over her chicks comforted me and gave me assurance that God loves me and my family. I imagined him carrying my daughter and protecting her. Though there was not much I could do for my daughter's situation, I could entrust her into his care.

Our answer may be delayed, but a delay is not denial. Because God loves us, he wants the best for you and me. He will never forget us, because we are his creations. Whatever battles we are dealing with, we can trust him. He will bring us through. Even though many delays often come because we don't cooperate with him right away, he will refine us in the process.

Rest assured God will never forget you. No trouble, persecution, distress, or anything else can separate us from the love of Jesus Christ (Romans 8:35).

Prayer

Lord, when the battles of life
threaten to leave me weary and overwhelmed,
remind me of your presence.
Thank you that I can rely
on your protection as a mother eagle.
Thank you for your deep and indescribable love for me.
Amen.

Hope
Waiting Expectantly

But Peter said,
"I don't have any silver or gold for you.
But I'll give you what I have.
In the name of Jesus Christ the Nazarene,
get up and walk!"
ACTS 3: 6 NLT

How long, Lord?

Sometimes I find myself asking this question. Waiting is difficult, especially with situations that linger without resolution. Do you have unresolved situations for which you are waiting on the Lord?

Acts 3 recounts the story of a man who was crippled from birth. This man waited all his life without hope of ever walking. He lay at the temple gate daily, begging. I assume a lot of temple worshippers knew him. Perhaps Peter had passed him many times before and never noticed him. But at God's appointed time, Peter noticed him and gave him the best gift of all. He said, "In the name of Jesus Christ of Nazareth, walk!" The man got up and walked. All the people saw him walking and praising God.

Though waiting can feel discouraging, the story of the crippled man provides hope. I imagine the crippled man showed up at the gate every day and didn't give in to self-pity. My daughter battled a health condition for over three years, and though we tried everything possible, nothing helped. While waiting, I made a conscious decision to show up daily and make the best of the opportunities God brought my way.

No matter the situation, you and I can trust God to come through for us. He is a God of *suddenly*. At the appointed time, the lame man found healing and walked. You will see God's manifestation in your situation in the fullness of time as you trust him. Can you praise God even now in your season of waiting?

Prayer

Lord, help me trust you
to work through my circumstances
and bring resolution in your time.
Thank you for giving me peace as I wait on you.
Amen.

Gratitude

The Power of Praise

Our God, will you not judge them?
For we have no power
to face this vast army that is attacking us.
We do not know what to do,
but our eyes are on you.

2 CHRONICLES 20:12

Do you know the saying "when it rains it pours?" A friend shared the African version with me while we were talking about how problems in life have a way of multiplying. She said, "When you are dealing with goats entering your house and trying to get rid of them, then you find out that sheep are on the roof and cows have broken out of the pen, not too far behind."

Do you have times when it feels like you are in the valley and the problems seem overwhelming? My goats, sheep, and cows in that season were teenage issues, marital and family conflicts, financial stress, health issues, and work deadlines. My family was stretched beyond our limits.

Jehoshaphat, king of Judah, could certainly relate. When he found out that the vast armies of Ammonites and Moabites were coming to attack Judah (2 Chronicles 20), his first response was to consult God. Then he proclaimed a fast for all Judah. He led the people in worship, and together they acknowledged God's sovereignty and power over the enemies. The king and all Judah cried out to the Lord in distress because they felt powerless to face the vast army.

In response to their cry, God promised to help them. He gave Jehoshaphat a strategy for the battle. The next day, King Jehoshaphat appointed men to lead the army. These men sang, "Give thanks to the Lord, for his love endures forever."

When the people praised God, something miraculous happened. Their enemies self-destroyed as they fought, and their dead bodies were scattered all over the battleground. Jehoshaphat and his army won the battle by singing praise to God.

Often, when we go through trials, we focus on the storm and the havoc they are causing, and we forget to praise God. Jehoshaphat reminds us to praise God and remember his goodness and faithfulness.

No matter the size of our storm, praise releases God's power to act on our behalf and causes the Enemy to self-destruct.

Prayer

There is power in praising you.
Help me remember your faithfulness
and lift my voice in praise.
Amen.

Rejoice in the Storm

Though the fig tree does not bud
and there are no grapes on the vines,
though the olive crop fails and the fields produce no food,
though there are no sheep in the pen
and no cattle in the stalls,
yet I will rejoice in the Lord,
I will be joyful in God my Savior.

HABAKKUK 3:17–18

The first time I read these verses in Habakkuk, I was perplexed and wondered how one could rejoice during great tragedies and trials.

When the prophet Habakkuk heard that an army would invade Israel and destroy it, he set his heart to focus on God's goodness. Rather than focus on the calamities to come, he focused on the truth of who God is regardless of the outcome. His stance was, if all else fails, if the crops don't yield a harvest, and if there are no sheep or cattle, he would still rejoice in the Lord.

How do we get through a storm with this attitude? Storms may rattle and shake us to the core, but like Habakkuk, we must predetermine to direct our heart and focus. We must choose to rejoice and remain triumphant in God regardless of our overwhelming circumstances.

It took ten years of dealing with relationship dysfunction and brokenness before I fully grasped this concept of joy despite the overwhelming circumstances. When we only focus on what's going on around us, we become depressed and filled with sorrow. But if we choose to see the sovereign hand and purpose of God in the storm, we will rejoice.

This type of joy does not come easily. We gain this joy as we abide with the Father in our trials and develop our relationship with him. During a recent trip to the emergency room, I noticed that I felt at peace and was not rattled by the situation. Instead, I prayed the names and attributes of God silently as I released the situation to him.

What do you do in a crisis when you don't know what to do?

Focus on the truth you know. Choosing to focus on our knowledge of God, rather than our circumstances, boosts our confidence, which ultimately produces joy.

Are you in the middle of a storm? Have faith in Christ, and believe the best is yet to come. The sovereign Lord is your strength.

Prayer

Lord, when the heat is turned on,
help me choose my attitude wisely and honor you.
Thank you for the power to rejoice in you
regardless of the situation.
In Jesus's name.
Amen.

Rejoice

Afterward you may go and celebrate
because of all the good things
the Lord your God has given to you and your household.

Deuteronomy 26:11 NLT

When I look back over the last ten years and recall what the Lord has done in my life, I rejoice because of all he has taught me. Many times I have determined to choose joy regardless of the situation.

It is difficult to ignore the negativity and flaming arrows the evil one shoots at us through our relationships with others. Sometimes our relationships are challenged because people refuse to own their blind spots. It can feel like there is an eight-hundred-pound elephant in the room, but everyone is choosing to pretend this elephant does not exist.

King Saul had unresolved issues and feelings of envy and jealousy toward David. In spite of those feelings, he wanted David to go along with his disillusions and pretense when, in reality, he had tried to kill David several times (1 Samuel 19:9–12).

Although Saul tried to mask his façade, David could see through it. Eventually, David ran away from Saul. While on the run, he encountered many obstacles, yet he depended on God to protect him. I believe David's mindset of joyful gratitude gave him favor with the Lord and victory over his enemies.

Like David, you and I have an Enemy whose main goal is to steal, kill, and destroy. His tactic is to steal our joy, especially in our relationships, and cause us to shift our focus from God's goodness to our woes and circumstances. He is responsible for quarrels, envy, bitterness, and jealousy in relationships.

How can we keep our joy and prevent the Enemy from messing with our relationships and stealing our joy?

We can frustrate him by bringing all our relationships to God in prayer and asking for wisdom in our interactions. We can recall the Lord's goodness over the years and choose to walk consistently in obedience while abiding in the shadow of the Almighty. We can confront in love and deliberately choose to rejoice.

What challenging relationships do you face today? How can you rejoice and trust that God is in control?

Prayer

Lord, thank you for all you have done for me.
Help me rejoice in you always, every day.
Amen.

Support

But the Lord was my support.

PSALM 18:18

Support staff are people who help keep an organization running smoothly. They take care of areas where we might fall short so we can focus on our main objectives. They make our lives easier. At work, my support includes the janitors who empty the trash and keep my office clean, my administrative team, and colleagues who help me stay organized and on top of my assignments. I am blessed with a great staff.

When life hits hard, where do you find support? In life, we all need it. I love the beautiful portrait the psalmist paints in Psalm 18. Let's take a look:

> He reached down from on high and took hold of me; he drew me out of deep waters. He rescued me from my powerful enemy, from my foes, who were too strong for me. They confronted me in the day of my disaster, but the Lord was my support. He brought me out into a spacious place; he rescued me because he delighted in me. (Psalm 18:16–19)

With God as my support, I have a tremendous advantage. He doesn't just help me stay organized and on track. He takes hold of me, draws me out of trouble, and protects me from powerful enemies. He also brings me to a spacious place where I have clarity, peace, and an overwhelming sense of his presence and love.

Do you need support? Do you need to experience God's mighty power? Reach out to him. His support is not available in stores or in employment agencies. No amount of money can purchase it. It is a precious gift available to us as children of God.

Why? Because God delights in you and me.

Friend, let that sink in. God delights in you, and he is ready to help you with whatever you need.

Prayer

Lord, I am in awe of your goodness
and amazing love for me.
Thank you for the gift of your precious support.
I bless you, Lord, for rescuing me
and bringing me into a spacious place.
Thank you for delighting in me.
Amen.

Home Invasion

But those who trust in the Lord
will find new strength.
They will soar high on wings like eagles.
They will run and not grow weary.
They will walk and not faint.

ISAIAH 40:31 NLT

In 2010 my family planned a trip to Orlando for Thanksgiving. During my time of fasting and prayers a few weeks before the trip, the Lord laid on my heart to pray about the trip. I wasn't sure exactly what to pray, but I asked the Lord to pray for us by his Spirit.

While packing for the trip, I felt I was to make copies of several hymns to sing on Thanksgiving Day before our meal. Throughout the week, this task was at the back of my mind. At the last minute, I made copies of the hymns.

We arrived in Orlando and settled in without any problems. On Thanksgiving Day, I cooked a meal for my family. While waiting to eat, I brought out the hymns and my Bible. We sang our hearts out to the Lord. Then we took turns and read Bible verses, prayed, and then shared our meal.

After the meal, the children went up to their room to play while I cleaned up the dishes and tidied the kitchen. When I finished, I wanted to lie down, but I kept hearing in my spirit, *Sit and watch TV with your husband.*

My husband dozed off in the chair, but I did not feel the release to leave, so I sat there and whispered prayers of thanksgiving to

God for my family.

Suddenly, I heard a sound as if someone was fiddling with the door lock. I went to the door and asked who it was. I could see a man and a woman through the peephole. The man unlocked our door. I pushed against the door with all my strength and held on to the lock mechanism. The man yelled, "Open this door! This is a home invasion!"

I started screaming for someone to call 911. The Lord infused me with strength and helped me hold on to the lock on the dead bolt.

Looking back, I see God's grace and mercy to thwart the Enemy's plans that day. He did not allow evil to befall my family. Through fasting and prayer, God sensitized me in the spirit to what he was doing and where he was working in our lives.

Ask the Lord to show you how you can deepen your relationship with him through fasting and prayer.

Prayer

Lord, you have done great things.
When I think about what could have happened
if the intruders had been successful,
I burst forth in praise.
You are a God of wonders.
You give strength to your people
and never let them be put to shame.
Thank you for filling me
with the wonder of your love and joy.
Amen.

Remember Your Word

Remember your word to your servant,
for you have given me hope.
PSALM 119:49

God often reveals his plans to us in a variety of ways. It could be through his Word, the Holy Spirit, dreams, or visions.

In my life I have noticed that God often speaks through dreams. It is one way the Lord prepares me for spiritual battle.

Years before our various troubles, I had many dreams about what was to come. In the dreams there was always someone coming to my rescue. In one dream, I saw a huge multicolored snake, about the size of an eighteen-wheeler. I prayed, and the snake turned away in slow motion. It took a long time for it to disappear.

I did not know the meaning of the dream, but it caused me to be vigilant and prayerful. I prayed and fasted for three days. I knew my family would face a major trial, but I could rely on God's help to bring us through. My family faced multiple trials for over ten years, but each time the Lord gave me a heads-up through dreams and the assurance of his presence.

God's revelations give us hope to stand firm in the storm. He revealed his plans for Joseph's life through dreams. God didn't hide his plans to destroy Sodom and Gomorrah from Abraham. He revealed many mysteries to Daniel. God's revelations to Daniel caused King Nebuchadnezzar to acknowledge the Lord. "Truly, your God is the greatest of gods, the Lord over kings, a revealer of mysteries, for you have been able to reveal this secret" (Daniel 2:47 NLT).

Remembering that the sovereign Lord never does anything until he reveals his plans to his servants (Amos 3:7) encourages my heart. As I remember this, hope and confidence arise in me. I can trust the Lord to fit me with the right gear and equipment for every battle.

Are you surrounded by a raging battle? What word has the Lord given you? Let hope arise in you as you remember the Lord's promises. Every word he gives you will come to pass. He is a faithful Father. The habit of remembering renews our hope and trust in the Lord.

Prayer

Lord, thank you for coming to my aid
and renewing my hope through your promises.
You are my fortress, stronghold, and deliverer,
a dependable shield where I take refuge.
Amen.

The Beauty of Jesus

One thing I ask from the Lord, this only do I seek:
that I may dwell in the house of the Lord
all the days of my life,
to gaze on the beauty of the Lord
and to seek him in his temple.

PSALM 27:4

As I prepared to travel for a family reunion, the song "Let the Beauty of Jesus Be Seen in Me" kept coming to mind. I wondered what the Lord was trying to tell me through the song.

Have you prayed for something and waited a long time for an answer? This family reunion was an answer to a long-awaited prayer, and this song was a reminder to abide in Christ and surrender my will to him during the family gathering.

The song played continuously at the back of my mind. I asked myself, *What is the beauty of Jesus?* Jesus's beauty is his holiness, power, and majesty. The beauty of Jesus is a beautiful expression of his gentleness, kindness, humility, long-suffering, faithfulness, self-discipline, compassion, righteousness, and purity (Galatians 5:22).

To behold the beauty of Jesus is to follow in his footsteps, walk like him, and follow his way of love. It means we glorify him in everything instead of pleasing ourselves. In being like Jesus, we share his love with others. The beauty of Jesus is not physical but an inner working of the Holy Spirit that leads to a transformed life. This transformation motivates us to be compassionate, bear with one another, show kindness, and to practice the fruit of the Spirit.

Our family was torn apart for over fifteen years by division, disunity, and dysfunction. This family reunion was a miracle. Brothers, uncles, aunties, moms, grandmas, and kids were reunited after a long time. Our children were excited to meet their cousins for the first time as they shared rides and walked through Disney World in Orlando. The adults enjoyed quiet moments together. Brothers sat at the dinner table and enjoyed sweet conversations that lasted into the early hours of the morning. Jesus's beauty shone in our interactions with one another. It was awesome to behold.

To reflect Jesus, we must have a relationship with him and remain in him. What does your relationship with Jesus and others look like?

Prayer

Dear Lord, thank you for restoring our family.
Thank you for nudging us to behold the beauty of Jesus.
This is difficult on our own,
but with your help we can do it.
We need your power to help us
reflect your beauty in our lives daily.
Amen.

Refined through Waiting

See, I have refined you, though not as silver;
I have tested you in the furnace of affliction.
ISAIAH 48:10

A friend and I met for coffee. Both of us experienced the death of our mothers about the same time, so this was a good opportunity to catch up. During our conversation, I said to my friend, "I feel like I am growing up." She asked me to tell her more. I shared about how I did not feel easily flustered anymore and how I have noticed that I am more patient. Waiting is no longer as hard as it used to be.

I like the prophet Micah's description of waiting. "But as for me, I watch in hope for the Lord, I wait for God my Savior; my God will hear me" (Micah 7:7). Watchful waiting is filled with expectation, anticipation, and trust in the Lord. It is waiting with confidence and firm assurance in God that deliverance will come.

Though the heat in the furnace seems unbearable, I wait in hope. Waiting has been a refiner's fire in my life. While waiting, I am encouraged that the Lord, the Creator of the universe, is working on my behalf to make all things, both good and bad, work together for my good. He is working behind the scenes on my heart and attitudes. He will refine my character.

Mary's song of praise was born out the furnace of affliction as she waited for the birth of Jesus.

My Soul glorifies the Lord
And my spirit rejoices in God my Savior,
      for he has been mindful
Of the humble state of his servant.
From now on, all generations will call me blessed
For the Mighty One has done great things for me—
Holy is his name. (Luke 1:46–49)

God never forsakes his children, especially when we experience the furnace of affliction. He controls the temperature as he works in us to act according to his good purpose. How have you experienced God in your season of waiting?

Prayer

Lord, waiting is a test of my faith.
Help me embrace my season of waiting
with a right heart attitude.
Refine me, Lord.
Amen.

How May I Serve You?

Unless the Lord had given me help,
I would soon have dwelt in the silence of death.

PSALM 94:17

What would you do if you received an unsolicited email with this in the subject line: *How may I serve you?* My initial response was caution. I looked at the name of the sender for clues. I thought maybe it was a scam.

I read the email:

> I don't know if this would help or not. We have a three-bedroom, one-and-a-half-story bath house that we rented out and are now trying to get cleaned and fixed up so we can sell it. Unfortunately, it is not furnished, so I don't know if it would work for you. If it works for you, you could stay there free, and we can delay putting it on the market.
>
> The house has been empty since October last year. So, it wouldn't be any trouble to wait a few more months before putting it on the market. We are replacing the dishwasher next weekend, but everything else is in working order. The house is in a great location, so you would at least have great neighbors. Please let us know if this would help or if there is anything else we can do.

Upon further investigation, I found out the email was from a friend of a friend who heard about our story. On July 5, 2015, my family became desperate. We had several storms in our area during that week. Lightning struck our home, and it caught on fire. We went from having a home to being homeless. This was another blow to our already fragile situation.

The timing of this email was divine intervention. We had exhausted all other options. We stayed at a hotel for a while until we ran out of funds. Some friends let us stay at their place when they went on vacation.

But then God intervened through the generosity of this couple who offered their place for us rent-free. On our first night at the house, my husband and I sat speechless for thirty minutes, each of us lost in our own thoughts. At some point, one of us prayed, and together we praised God for his grace and mercies toward our family.

The scope, nature, and size of our storm is no barrier to a God-sized miracle. Friend, whatever storms you face, know that God is with you. He will provide at just the right time.

Prayer

Lord, we can never make it without you.
During a low point in our lives when all hope was gone,
you showed us mercy and grace.
You provided through others
who loved and served us beyond our imagination.
Thank you, Lord, for loving my family.
Amen.

My Refuge

Have mercy on me, O God, have mercy!
I look to you for protection.
I will hide beneath the shadow of your wings
until the danger passes by.
PSALM 57:1 NLT

Under the shadow of your wings
Most High
My soul finds rest
Through the tempest and the storm
Under your wings
I safely abide
And find peace for my soul
Your love anchors my soul.

The storms rage
The water is over my head
But you hold me still
Under your wings
Like a mother hen
You cover me
As you sweep me
Under your wing.

You faithfully hold me
Through the storm

Under your wings
You are working
All for my good
To fulfill your purpose
Under your wings.

Angels surround me
You rebuke my enemy
Your love surrounds me
I feel your presence
Under your wings
Safe, secure, at rest
I smile at the storm.

Prayer

Heavenly Father, I exalt your name.
I am grateful that through the storms, pains, and tears,
you were there to guide
and provide protection and hope.
If I had a thousand tongues,
they would not be enough to express my gratitude.
Thank you for providing a haven under your wings
and for sustaining me
through the fiercest storms of my life.
I love you, Lord.
Amen.

Hidden Treasures

And I will give you treasures
hidden in the darkness—secret riches.
I will do this so you may know
that I am the Lord, the God of Israel,
the one who calls you by name.

ISAIAH 45:3 NLT

Even though King Cyrus of Persia was a pagan, God chose him to accomplish his purpose of liberating Israel from oppression by the Babylonians. Because of his obedience, God promised to give Cyrus the rich treasures of Babylon, which were stored in secret places (Isaiah 45:3).

God is sovereign, and he can bring hope to a hopeless situation by choosing an unlikely person as his messenger. We will all go through trials, afflictions, oppression, and persecution in life. These challenges compel us to recognize our inadequacies and need for God.

For many years, I was a self-sufficient and driven woman. I was a wife and mom to four kids, worked full time, and ran our home as best I could. I included God in my life by attending church regularly. I prayed, read Scripture daily, and served as a deacon at my church. I led a women's Bible study once a month. My life was out of balance, and though I was doing the right things, my motives and attitudes were not always aligned with God's will and purpose for my life.

When adversity hit and I faced multiple trials, I could only see devastation and ruin. But as I leaned on God and asked for his help, he showed me glimpses of treasures and hidden riches.

My first treasure was gaining God's perspective and seeing what he could accomplish through my trials. During this dark season, I received the precious treasure of intimacy and abiding with God at a deeper level as he revealed his truths and opened my heart to receive them.

I experienced his faithfulness and deep personal care. I was forgiven for my negative attitudes, resentment, and bitterness. I also received hope and embraced my identity in Christ.

But the best treasure of the dark season was experiencing God's love personally. It was no longer an abstract concept. Along with that came his peace and joy. Friend, these riches of dark, secret places surpass all earthly wealth—silver, gold, or diamonds.

Without going through the difficult and dark times, I would not appreciate the power of Jesus to pull me out of the mud and mire. I have come a long way from knowing *about* God to *experiencing* him and possessing his riches of mercy, forgiveness, comfort, deliverance, love, and victory in Jesus.

Friend, will you trust God to reveal the hidden treasures in your trials? He specializes in helping us uncover hidden treasures in our adversities. He is doing a new thing. Do you perceive it?

Prayer

Lord, our trials have a purpose
if we will let you show us.
Thank you for the hidden treasures in my trials,
because through them I will experience
your mercy, love, grace, and deliverance.
Amen.

Show Gratitude by Comforting Others

He comforts us in all our troubles
so that we can comfort others.
When they are troubled,
we will be able to give them
the same comfort God has given us.

2 CORINTHIANS 1:4 NLT

Mary had an encounter that transformed her life. She was from Magdala, a small village on the shore of the Sea of Galilee. Mary suffered from demon possession, and these evil spirits dominated her for many years. She was not in control of her mind. We don't know the cause of her demon possession, but one thing is clear: when Mary Magdalene met Jesus, she was completely delivered and healed.

That encounter changed her life forever. She regained her mind and was no longer held back by the chains of demonic oppression. To show her gratitude, she became a devout follower of Jesus. Mary is mentioned fourteen times in the gospels, most often in connection with other women who had also been healed of evil spirits. She was among a band of women who traveled with Jesus and supported him and his disciples with their own resources (Luke 8:3).

How have you experienced God's comfort and deliverance in your storm? Our challenges are springboards of hope that provide an opportunity to draw closer to God and serve others.

Whatever pain you have experienced in life will become a source of inspiration to offer hope and encouragement to others. Mary and another woman were the first to see the resurrected Jesus. He sent them to inform the disciples that he had risen from the dead. (Matthew 28:2–10). Imagine Mary's excitement as she shared the news with the disciples: "I have seen the Lord!" (John 20:18). Now, picture their joy as they received this good news from Mary.

You and I can use the gifts from adversity as stepping-stones to inspire others. As a result of allowing Jesus to transform my adversity and brokenness, I now share my message of hope through writing, speaking, mentoring, and leading a women's small group at my church.

Who needs your encouragement? How will you inspire others? With God's help, you can turn your adversity into a beautiful purpose.

Prayer

Lord, your love and mercy
are the glue that holds my broken pieces together.
Thank you for changing me.
Help me move from pain
to pursue your beautiful purpose for my life.
Thank you for the opportunity to comfort others.
Amen.

Give Thanks

Be thankful in all circumstances,
for this is God's will for you who belong to Christ Jesus.
1 Thessalonians 5:18 NLT

For as long as I can remember, gratitude has been a part of my life. Expressing gratitude comes naturally because of my name, *Temitope*, which means *this is enough to thank God*.

Our expression of gratitude can be superficial and done out of obligation. Paul models for us gratitude from the heart that does not depend on external circumstances. In many of the New Testament letters, Paul began his letters with phrases such as "We give thanks for you" or "I always thank my God when I pray for you." Paul was in prison when he wrote these letters to the churches.

In Philippians, Paul expresses his thankfulness to the church in Philippi for their financial support. How could Paul be thankful while he was unjustly imprisoned? His secret was thankfulness and contentment in all situations.

> Not that I was ever in need, for I have learned how to be content with whatever I have. I know how to live on almost nothing or with everything. I have learned the secret of living in every situation, whether it is with a full stomach or empty, with plenty or little. For I can do everything through Christ, who gives me strength. (Philippians 4:11–13 NLT)

When we give thanks, we are celebrating and acknowledging

God's goodness and sovereignty over our situation. Gratitude is like applying WD-40 to a rusty door that will not open. Thankfulness has a way of giving us perspective and easing our pain as we wait on the Lord.

When we embrace God's perspective, gratitude flows from our heart and influences our attitudes and responses to life's challenges. We experience the type of joy that Paul expressed in Philippians. We appreciate the people the Lord places in our lives and see his hand in our interactions and relationships.

Do you want to experience joy in adversity? In what ways will you rely on God for strength to be thankful for your situation?

Prayer

Father, I acknowledge my discontent
with my situation and ask for your help.
I desire a new heart attitude.
Help me embrace contentment
and give thanks in all things.
Amen.

The Gift of Peace

I am leaving you with a gift—
peace of mind and heart. And the peace I give
is a gift the world cannot give.
So don't be troubled or afraid.

JOHN 14:27

Ms. Pearl had a special gift as an encourager. She made everyone around her smile and laugh as she told clean, funny jokes. I have many fond memories from hanging out with her on the deacon board and during prayer times in her home. She made each person feel special.

During a time of hymn singing, the pastor asked Ms. Pearl to pick a hymn. With a twinkle in her eye, she pointed and said, "I will take him, him, and him." We had a good laugh, and then she chose "It is Well with My Soul," by Horatio Spafford.

Even if Ms. Pearl had any struggles, it was hard to tell because of her positive and joyful attitude. When she was diagnosed with cancer, she encouraged others while maintaining an attitude of peace and thankfulness. She recognized that she would not be around for much longer. During her last moments with her family, she encouraged each of them, and just before she passed on, she said, "I lived a good life. With the Lord's help, I made the best of it."

Those who sow in peace will reap a harvest of righteousness (James 3:18). I believe Ms. Pearl is doing that in heaven along with the other saints who have gone ahead of us. When Jesus was about to leave this world to return to the Father, he was not worried about himself. He encouraged his disciples and left them with the gift of peace, the kind that the world cannot offer. I am amazed at Jesus's great love and compassion for his followers. Because of his sacrifice on the cross, we have his peace and victory.

In this world, we will have many trials and sorrows. In what ways, have you experienced God's peace in your trials? How can you express your gratitude and encourage others?

Prayer

Lord, may I hold on to your peace
and trust you in difficult times.
When I am worried and anxious,
please flood my heart with your peace,
and help me worship and meditate on your Word.
Thank you, Jesus, for blessing me with your peace.
Amen.

A Beautiful Mess

He has made everything beautiful in its time.
ECCLESIASTES 3:11

The power was out, and there was total darkness. It was a very frightening night I will never forget. Hurricane Fran wreaked havoc and caused major damage in North Carolina in 1996. The hurricane destroyed homes. Power lines were down. Century-old trees covered the ground like matchsticks. Throughout the night there was howling wind, rain, and more wind.[8]

While lying in bed, I recited Psalm 23 several times and prayed fervently. I asked the Lord to protect my family and others in our neighborhood. It was scary to hear the howling wind and trees popping and falling.

When morning came, there was a mess everywhere. Trees fell over houses and on the streets and driveways. It was as if a massive agent of destruction went through our neighborhood with a bulldozer.

In all, Fran caused thirty-seven deaths, twenty-four of which were in North Carolina. She caused 7.2 billion dollars in damages. When I saw all the downed trees and debris in my neighborhood, all I could see was a mess.

Like the mess from hurricane Fran, when you and I reflect on our struggles and challenges, we probably see a mess. But when Jesus sees our mess, he sees a beautiful mess. He sees what we can become, and he sees the good he can bring out of our chaos. The Samaritan woman in John 4 was a hopeless mess. She felt unworthy as she hopped from one man to another. But when Jesus met her, he offered her living water, and she accepted. Her encounter with Jesus turned her messy life into a beautiful message, and many in her hometown believed because of her testimony.

In God's hands, your struggles—heartaches, financial troubles, a health crisis, prodigals, and marital problems—can become beautiful messes as he works all things together for your good and for his glory. He makes all things beautiful in his time.

Prayer

Help me trust you with my messy situations.
Thank you for all the ways you are working
behind the scenes
to make all things beautiful in your time.
I praise and bless you, Lord.
Amen.

A Closing Blessing

Although the storms of life may
Beat heavily against you,
May you release your worries
And trust the Everlasting God to give you
A crown of beauty for your ashes,
Oil of joy instead of mourning,
And a garment of praise instead of despair.
May you embrace hope and stand strong in your faith.
May you be like a great oak, planted by the Lord
As a display of his splendor.
May the favor of the Lord rest upon you,
As you lean on him and he walks with you on your journey.
God bless.

Endnotes

1. Henry Kamm, "Pope Meets in Jail with His Attacker," *New York Times,* Dec. 28, 1983, https://www.nytimes.com/1983/12/28/world/pope-meets-in-jail-with-his-attacker.html.

2. Bob Meisner, Audrey Meisner, and Stephen W. Nance, *Marriage Under Cover: Thriving in a Culture of Quiet Desperation* (MileStones International Publishers, Huntsville, Alabama, 2005).

3. Immaculée Ilibagiza and Steve Erwin, *Left to Tell: Discovering God Amidst the Rwandan Holocaust* (Hay House Inc., Carlsbad, California, 2016), 73–94.

4. Corrie ten Boom and Jamie Buckingham, *Tramp for the Lord* (Berkeley Publishing Company, New York, New York, 2011), 53.

5. Jim Puzzanghera, "Shocked into Reality by the Great Recession," *Los Angeles Times*, June 27, 2014, http://www.latimes.com/business/la-fi-recession-psyche-20140627-story.html.

6. Lydia DePillis, "My Road Back from the Great Recession," *CNN Business*, January 3, 2018 https://money.cnn.com/2018/01/03/news/economy/recession-stories/index.html.

7. Lee Strobel and Leslie Strobel, *Surviving a Spiritual Mismatch in Marriage* (Zondervan, Grand Rapids Michigan, 2002), 29–41.

8. Martha Quillin, "20 Years Later People in NC Still Remember the Night Hurricane Fran Tore Up the State," *The News & Observer*, September 6, 2016, http://www.newsobserver.com/news/local/article99266457.html.

Order Information

To order additional copies of this book, please visit
www.redemption-press.com.
Also available on Amazon.com and
BarnesandNoble.com,
or by calling toll-free (844) 2REDEEM (273-3336).

CPSIA information can be obtained
at www.ICGtesting.com
Printed in the USA
LVHW111912041119
636282LV00007B/1136/P